D0929902

DEVELOPMENT CENTRE STUDIES

JAPAN'S GENERAL TRADING COMPANIES

MERCHANTS OF ECONOMIC DEVELOPMENT

BY

KIYOSHI KOJIMA AND TERUTOMO OZAWA

DEVELOPMENT CENTRE
OF THE ORGANISATION FOR ECONOMIC CO-OPERATION AND DEVELOPMENT

Pursuant to article 1 of the Convention signed in Paris on 14th December, 1960, and which came into force on 30th September, 1961, the Organisation for Economic Co-operation and Development (OECD) shall promote policies designed:

- to achieve the highest sustainable economic growth and employment and a rising standard of living in Member countries, while maintaining financial stability, and thus to contribute to the development of the world economy;
- to contribute to sound economic expansion in Member as well as non-member countries in the process of economic development; and
- to contribute to the expansion of world trade on a multilateral, non-discriminatory basis in accordance with international obligations.

The Signatories of the Convention on the OECD are Austria, Belgium, Canada, Denmark, France, the Federal Republic of Germany, Greece, Iceland, Ireland, Italy, Luxembourg, the Netherlands, Norway, Portugal, Spain, Sweden, Switzerland, Turkey, the United Kingdom and the United States. The following countries acceded subsequently to this Convention (the dates are those on which the instruments of accession were deposited): Japan (28th April, 1964), Finland (28th January, 1969), Australia (7th June, 1971) and New Zealand (29th May, 1973).

The Socialist Federal Republic of Yugoslavia takes part in certain work of the OECD (agreement of 28th October, 1961).

The Development Centre of the Organisation for Economic Co-operation and Development was established by decision of the OECD Council on 23rd October, 1962.

The purpose of the Centre is to bring together the knowledge and experience available in Member countries of both economic development and the formulation and execution of general policies of economic aid; to adapt such knowledge and experience to the actual needs of countries or regions in the process of development and to put the results at the disposal of the countries by appropriate means.

The Centre has a special and autonomous position within the OECD which enables it to enjoy scientific independence in the execution of its task. Nevertheless, the Centre can draw upon the experience and knowledge available in the OECD in the development field.

Publié en français sous le titre :

**LES SOCIÉTÉS JAPONAISES
DE COMMERCE GÉNÉRAL**
LEUR RÔLE DANS LE DÉVELOPPEMENT ÉCONOMIQUE

The present study was undertaken in conjunction with the Development Centre's research project on "New Forms of Investment in Developing Countries". This project was initiated in 1980 as part of the Centre's research programme on Interdependence and Development.

Also available

INTERNATIONAL SUBCONTRACTING – A New Form of Investment by Dimitri
Germidis (January 1981)
(41 80 08 1) ISBN 92-64-12129-3 228 pages   £5.40   US$13.50   F54.00

**NEW FORMS OF INTERNATIONAL INVESTMENT IN DEVELOPING
COUNTRIES** by Charles Oman
(41 84 02 1) ISBN 92-64-12590-6 140 pages   £6.50   US$13.00   F65.00

Prices charged at the OECD Publications Office.

*THE OECD CATALOGUE OF PUBLICATIONS and supplements will be sent free of charge
on request addressed either to OECD Publications Office,
2, rue André-Pascal, 75775 PARIS CEDEX 16, or to the OECD Sales Agent in your country.*

TABLE OF CONTENTS

Acknowledgements

Our work on the overseas investment activities of Japan's general trading companies (sogo shosha) started in the early summer of 1981 as part of the research project organised by the Development Centre of the OECD on the "new forms" of investment in developing countries. Japanese overseas investments are known to exhibit a relatively high incidence of minority ownership and the non-equity type of investment referred to as the new forms. Since the general trading companies are Japan's leading overseas investors, it behooved us to find out to what extent, in what ways, and why they are engaged in the new forms in their overseas investment activities.

In the course of writing this report we have become heavily indebted to Dr. Charles Oman for his intellectual leadership and constant encouragement. We are also grateful to Dr. Henry Ergas and Mr. Derek Rooken Smith for their useful comments on an earlier draft.

Kiyoshi Kojima
Terutomo Ozawa

PREFACE

The spectacular growth and development of tne Japanese economy has brought increasing worldwide attention in recent years to Japan's unique economic institutions. One of those institutions, which has clearly played a major role in the country's postwar economic success, is the <u>sogo shosha</u>, or general trading company. These trading companies have also been in the forefront of Japan's rapidly growing trade and investment activities in developing countries.

In 1980, the Development Centre embarked on a research project on "New Forms of International Investment in Developing Countries" (1). The first phase of this project, now completed, relies to a considerable extent on data and analyses from a number of developing countries which host such investment. The second phase, now getting underway, will examine the new forms of investment in developing countries from the perspective of investors' home countries.

The present study was undertaken by Professors Kojima and Ozawa in conjunction with the first phase of this project; but it may be regarded as the first major result of the second phase, in that it draws extensively on knowledge available only in Japan regarding the overseas activities of the country's top nine trading companies. Not only does the study provide a timely and in-depth response to the growing interest in the trading companies as an institution in their own right. By identifying ana analysing the trading companies' varied traae and investment activities in developing countries, the study makes a unique and important contribution to our understanding of Japanese firms' use of new forms of investment in those countries. And by explaining the evolution of the trading companies' role as the Japanese economy developed in the postwar period, the study points to important implications for today's developing countries which may wish to emulate or benefit from the Japanese experience.

As such, this study ought to be of particular interest to policy makers and their advisers in developing countries. But it is also recommended for the international audience more generally.

Just Faaland
President of the OECD
Development Centre

September, 1984

Chapter I

FROM INSTANT NOODLES TO MISSILES

International trade is Japan's lifeline, and the general trading companies, or sogo shosha, have played a unique role in maintaining it. Their trading activities are extremely diversified, ranging "from instant noodles to missiles", as the popular saying goes in Japan. Indeed, they have been so successful that their contribution to Japan's impressive industrialisation is now being recognised both at home and abroad.

Oddly enough, the activities of these trading companies at once reflect the former backwardness of the Japanese economy and its present resilience and strength. As part and parcel of the modernisation programme that Japan embarked upon in the mid-19th century, trading companies were fostered to connect the resource-poor, industrially backward country with the rest of the world, upon which it depended for its imports of natural resources. This was the only way for Japan to keep its workshops operating and to export manufactured products in order to earn the necessary foreign exchange.

Over and beyond raw materials and energy resources, the companies were also instrumental in bringing home advanced Western machinery and equipment as well as information about new technologies. Without all this, Japan's successful industrialisation could never have come about. And this is one of the major reasons why developing countries in particular are interested in learning about this distinctive Japanese institution, for similar instruments could be fashioned for their own economic development.

Indeed, trading companies can be a vital tool for an outward-oriented strategy of industrialisation. Initially, Japan's trading companies were designed as import-export agents for manufacturing firms, and especially small- and medium-sized ones, so that they could concentrate on production without dispersing scarce human and financial resources to set up their own trading facilities. International marketing and procurement activities, together with such trade-supportive activities as trade financing, market research, warehousing and shipping, thus came to be performed by trading companies. These activities can be considered as infrastructural services that support manufacturing activities. In other words, a division of corporate functions between manufacturing firms engaged in "directly productive" activities and trading firms engaged in "transactional" activities was to become a distinctive feature of the Japanese economy. Early on, this small and resource-indigent country had to learn the intricacies of, and develop capacities for, foreign trade as a matter of national survival.

11

Nowadays, highly integrated modern corporations are capable of providing from within (that is, of internalising) all trading and trade-supportive services. When they venture abroad as multinationals, they usually set up wholly- or majority-owned operations to take advantage of their own business infrastructures which, added to their core of manufacturing activities, create self-contained industrial enclaves in the local host economy.

There has been widespread resistance to this latter (or "old") form of investment on the part of developing host countries. At present they are striving to purchase corporate resources in as "unbundled" a form as is practical. As a result, the traditional form of investment is being broken up into a variety of new forms of business involvement, which the developing countries then have re-packaged into an operation with as much participation and control as possible. The so-called "new" forms of investment (1) -- minority-foreign-owned joint ventures and such non-equity types of business arrangements as technical-assistance agreements, managerial and marketing contracts, licensing, turnkey operations, production-sharing and the like -- are more and more frequently arranged, either alongside or in lieu of the traditional type of investment in developing countries.

It is against this backdrop that the general trading companies have become increasingly involved as investors in developing countries, for they can provide new arrangements for a variety of business infrastructures. (In fact, this is one reason why some developing countries themselves are eager to foster their own trading companies.) Resource-rich developing countries, for example, are pursuing resource-based industrialisation; for this large-scale extractive ventures must be organised and financed and access to markets in resource-importing industrialised countries assured. These ventures often turn into regional economic development projects fully supported and subsidised not only by the developing countries themselves but also by the industrialised countries as part of their economic co-operation programmes.

As Japan is almost completely dependent on overseas resources, it has been particularly active in this type of project. The general trading companies quickly established themselves as effective project organiser/co-ordinators by providing a multitude of supportive business services, ranging from project financing and supervision, procurement of plant facilities and construction of physical infrastructures (such as ports and highways) to marketing of extracted resources and consulting services. As we will discuss later on, trading companies have also become involved in non-extractive regional development programmes, such as the construction of airports, tourist facilities and housing complexes in developing countries.

Labour-abundant developing countries, on the other hand, are interested in attracting relatively labour-intensive manufacturing ventures. Export processing zones, for example, are offered as an inducement to foreign manufacturers. Small- and medium-sized ventures are particularly welcome in developing countries, since they tend to bring in relatively more labour-intensive, locally congruent technologies and create a more competitive industrial environment than large-scale, capital-intensive ventures. In response, a large number of relatively small-scale ventures have been launched by Japan's trading companies, especially in Asia, in partnership with local interests. Indeed, some 80 per cent of their manufacturing ventures abroad are concentrated in developing countries.

Today most developing countries are burdened with heavy external debts and yet remain committed to industrialisation. They are therefore in dire need of earning foreign exchange by exporting whatever they can manage to sell abroad. Some are even imposing counter-purchase requirements, especially when they import industrial machinery and plants. (The Communist countries have long been known as countertrade practitioners.) It is this increased use of countertrade that is compelling many heavy machinery producers in the West, particularly in the United States, to create their own trading companies: General Electric, Rockwell International and General Motors have all set up trading companies recently. Here, Japan's general trading companies, with their worldwide marketing networks, have without doubt found themselves better prepared to meet this new demand from developing countries, making Japan's international trade even more resilient.

All these recent developments have put the general trading companies in the limelight. They are finding new business opportunities -- and taking on heavy responsibilities and risks in the process -- in commercial transactions related to the developing countries' drive for economic development. This "pull" effect on the trading companies to "internationalise" their business operations has come at an opportune moment, for their domestic operations have waned considerably in recent years and they have had to look abroad for new business opportunities.

The recent decline in their domestic business has been caused for the most part by a rapid structural shift in Japan's manufacturing activities. During the early postwar period, trading companies made a significant contribution to Japan's exports of relatively standardized manufactures, such as steel, textiles and sundries. But with the growth of more sophisticated and highly differentiated consumer-goods industries, notably automobiles and electronics products, dependence on the trading companies began to decline as manufacturers set up their own sales networks overseas. (In Japan this development is dubbed the "departure-from-traders" phenomenon.) In fact, this decline led to a belief that the trading companies would gradually become less and less useful and would eventually die out, a belief popularised in the so-called "demise theory". Yet this prediction proved to be premature: although their role as export agents for Japanese manufacturers diminished, the trading companies started to increase third-country or offshore trade intermediation (now popularly identified as the "departure-from-Japan" phenomenon).

Moreover, their role as import agents continued to expand as Japan became ever more dependent on overseas resources. By combining their traditional functions -- intermediary, financial, and information-gathering -- into a synergic function, the general trading companies have turned into overseas project organisers for large-scale ventures in resource and regional development. Moreover, they have come to play a key role in helping Japanese manufacturers, and particularly small- and medium-sized enterprises, set up shop in labour-abundant developing countries to produce technologically-mature, labour-intensive products by investing jointly and providing needed infrastructural services. All these activities are thus giving the trading companies a new lease of life.

By a curious twist of fate, the fact that the trading companies were "pushed out" of Japan by internal structural changes and were forced to turn outward into new forms of investment is proving to suit them better than the old form as a way to multinationalise their business operations. True, as we will see in this study, they do set up wholly-owned trading subsidiaries (i.e., the old form of investment) abroad, but their ventures in such non-commerce sectors as manufacturing and resource extraction are, as a rule, minority-owned joint ventures. In these sectors, the trading companies, unlike manufacturers, seldom possess any firm-specific production technology, such as patents or process know-how, that needs to be internalised in their own organisational operations in order for them to extract monopoly rents. In essence, their corporate advantage is their ability to organise, co-ordinate and intermediate market transactions, as will be shown in the following chapters.

A BRIEF OUTLINE

The primary purpose of this study is to examine the overseas investment activities of Japan's general trading companies, particularly those of the "Top Nine", and to pinpoint their major characteristics. In this way, we will be able to assess the significance of the new forms of operation in their overseas investment and examine the implications for developing host countries.

Chapter II presents a brief historical account of the birth and growth of the general trading companies, describes their overall functions and shows how their drive for multinational operations was generated. The three traditional functions of the Top Nine companies -- transaction intermediation, information-gathering and quasi-banking -- and how these functions combined to create a new synergic function, namely an organiser/co-ordinator function, are examined.

The following chapters are concerned with their overseas investments. For this purpose, investment activities have been divided into four major areas: trading networks, manufacturing, resource development and non-trade service ventures. The Top Nine trading companies' investments in overseas trading networks are examined in Chapter III. In this connection, a typology of their ventures is introduced, in which ventures are broken down into eight different types. The same typology is used throughout the rest of the study to facilitate our analysis. Chapter IV focusses on manufacturing ventures, Chapter V on resource development ventures and Chapter VI on non-trade service ventures. Chapter VII presents an overall assessment and draws conclusions. The Annex evaluates the existing body of direct investment theories in the light of the trading companies' experiences with the new forms of investment.

SCOPE OF STUDY

Our study covers the overseas ventures of Japan's Top Nine trading companies and those business activities that are closely linked to their overseas investment, namely third-country trade intermediation, overseas direct loans and plant exports on a turnkey or product-in-hand basis, which serve as a major vehicle for technology transfers to developing countries.

The Top Nine trading companies' overseas ventures were examined and sorted out in our statistical compilation on a comparative basis. Included were 292 ventures for Mitsui & Co., 278 ventures for Mitsubishi Corporation, 215 ventures for Marubeni Corporation, 217 ventures for C. Itoh & Co., 130 ventures for Sumitomo Corporation, 111 ventures for Nissho-Iwai, 99 ventures for Tomen, 75 ventures for Kanematsu Gosho and 81 ventures for Nichimen Jitsugyo -- that is, a total of 1 498 ventures. They represent practically all the overseas ventures that had been set up by the nine traders by the end of March 1980 (the end of fiscal 1979 in Japan). Yet these figures inevitably include a number of ventures -- albeit very few -- that were either closed temporarily or already out of business at that time (e.g., the ventures set up in Iran and some Central American and African countries). These ventures were purposely kept in the study, partly because of a lack of clear-cut information about their fate and more importantly because our purpose is, after all, to study the behavioural pattern of the trading companies' investment activities, past and present.

The total figures in our statistical tables should be interpreted with caution, for some ventures are jointly owned by two or more trading companies, as is often the case with, say, resource extractive ventures. Thus double counting is involved to some extent. Strictly speaking, the total should be construed as the number of investment participations by individual trading companies rather than the total number of overseas firms in which they invested.

To carry out our task we have drawn upon the quantitative information contained in Kaigai Shinshutsu Kigyo Soran ("Japanese Multinationals. Facts and Figures", Oriental Economist, Tokyo, 1981), Kigyobetsu Kaigai Toshi ("Overseas Investments by Enterprises", Keizai Chosa Kyokai, Tokyo, 1982), and other documents. We collected "qualitative" and "in-house" information by means of interviews with personnel in the trading companies. Since the situations of -- and hence the statistics on -- overseas ventures are constantly changing, some of the information gathered for our study may already be either obsolete or inappropriate in the light of more recent developments. It is, however, our hope and belief that the general trends and patterns, if not the minute details, in this study will remain sufficiently valid to delineate the salient characteristics of the general trading companies' overseas ventures and related activities.

Chapter II

ANATOMY OF THE GENERAL TRADING COMPANIES

Few people outside Japan realise that the general trading companies are the country's leading multinationals, not only in overseas trading but also in manufacturing, resource extraction and other non-trading ventures. In 1979, for example, Mitsui & Co., Mitsubishi Corporation, Marubeni Corporation, and C. Itoh & Co. were the four largest Japanese investors. Sumitomo Corporation occupied sixth position, Nissho-Iwai came in ninth, Tomen eleventh, Kanematsu Gosho nineteenth and Nichimen Jitsugyo twenty-fourth (see table on following page). Thus the Top Nine trading companies were all among Japan's 25 largest overseas investors. In fact, they accounted for more than half of the total value as well as of the total number of outstanding overseas investments made by Japan's top 50 multinationals. On the Top One Hundred list of Japan's multinationals, three other less well-known trading companies are included: Toyota Tsusho (69th), Nomura Trading Co. (84th) and Kawatetsu Shoji (95th).

The fact that the trading companies are active investors in non-commerce sectors such as manufacturing and resource extraction may surprise those who regard trading companies basically as commercial go-betweens in wholesale business. Why do these traders, they may ask, have to invest so much in so many different non-commercial ventures? The question is appropriate, for the multi-nationalisation of the trading companies' operations is definitely a postwar -- and indeed a relatively recent -- phenomenon. In order to fully understand this development, it is necessary to examine their origins and functions in the Japanese economy and analyse how their multinationalisation has come about.

Trading companies' business can be best defined as intermediation in space and time, for these two factors create the myriad uncertainties and risks associated with supply and demand. The larger the geographical space economic activities span, the greater the barriers to communications (different languages and customs) and transportation (the availability of appropriate modes of transportation) and the greater the need for warehousing. Similarly, the longer it takes to complete economic transactions, the greater the risks involved, mainly in the form of unforeseen changes and gaps in supply-and-demand conditions.

Trading companies, the willing bearers of, and capitalisers on, these uncertainties and risks, perform three primary functions: (1) transaction intermediation; (2) financial intermediation (or quasi-banking); and

(3) information-gathering. Some auxiliary functions, such as transport logistics (dealing with space) and warehousing (bridging time), are also performed simultaneously. In addition, trading companies have recently learned how to combine all these primary and auxiliary functions into an organiser/coordinator function, a synergic function whose effectiveness is much greater than the sum of its components.

HOW THE TRADING COMPANIES RANK AMONG
JAPAN'S TOP 25 MULTINATIONAL CORPORATIONS (1979)

RANKING	CORPORATION	Cumulative value value of investment in Yen 100 mn.*
1	°Mitsui & Co.	2 353
2	°Mitsubishi Corporation	1 581
3	°Marubeni Corporation	1 552
4	°C. Itoh & Co.	1 262
5	Japan Asahan Aluminium	870
6	°Sumitomo Corporation	688
7	Matsushita Electric Industries	674
8	Nissan Motor	596
9	°Nissho-Iwai	569
10	Toray	568
11	°Tomen	478
12	Honda Motor	439
13	Kawasaki Steel	422
14	Sanyo Electric	386
15	Shin Nihon Steel	381
16	Sony	376
17	Mitsubishi Heavy Industries	353
18	Ishikawajima-Harima Heavy Industries	350
19	°Kanematsu Gosho	340
20	Japan Usiminus	325
21	Kawasaki Heavy Industries	314
22	Tokyo Kyuku Dentetsu	300
23	Teijin	293
24	°Nichimen Jitsugyo	289
25	Tokyo Shibaura Electric	282

*   To estimate the dollar equivalent, the most convenient conversion rate is 200 Yen per dollar

°   Trading company

Source: Compiled from Toyo Keizai, Kaigai Shinshutsu Kigyo Soran (Japanese Multinationals Facts and Figures), Tokyo, 1981, p. 10.

THE RISE OF THE GREAT COMPANIES

Many Japanese trading companies have long and colourful histories. The House of Mitsui (now Mitsui & Co.) opened its first shop as long ago as 1616, although its "modern" form of organisation dates from 1874, when it set up a trading network of 27 branch offices throughout Japan. "The major products handled were rice, tea and processed marine products, and business was conducted strictly on a commission basis" (2). Another great house, Mitsubishi, was founded in 1875 by a lowly samurai named Yataro Iwasaki (who was actually the son of a peasant but bought a low-ranking samurai title).

Interestingly enough, the House of Sumitomo, which was established by a priest turned herbalist about 400 years ago and whose major source of income was Japan's largest copper mine, did not have and, in fact, did not allow a trading company to be set up until after World War II, because its founder had been firmly against commercial speculation. Abhorrence of commerce had been handed down as an unbreakable house decree until 1945 when Sumitomo Shoji (now Sumitomo Corporation) was set up, and even then it was primarily to provide employment opportunities for those Sumitomo workers who, either because they had been engaged in war-related production at home or had returned from their overseas assignment, were out of work at the end of the war (3).

These famous houses, as well as others, had all grown rapidly during the early Meiji period (1868-1912), when the Japanese Government made it a national imperative to industrialise the economy and modernise social institutions. This was the period in which Japan's famed zaibatsu groups came into existence, as an outgrowth of the big mercantile houses. The rise of the zaibatsu was a pragmatic match of historical accident and intentional public policy. In the mid-19th century, confronted with the enormous task of building a prosperous nation and a strong army, Japan had to mobilise and make the best possible use of scarce key resources, such as human skills and capital. In this very early stage of economic development, and with a sense of national urgency, Japan found it necessary to concentrate economic resources either in the state -- as is done currently by many developing nations -- or in the hands of a few private entrepreneurial groups, in a manner analogous to the rationalised "natural or legal monopoly" designed to allow scale economies (4). Japan chose the second alternative. Although the government took the initiative in building modern plants with the assistance of hired Western engineers and technicians, the plants soon were sold to private interests, the mercantile houses (5). It was against the backdrop of this national imperative that a handful of great mercantile families moved to the forefront of Japan's economic modernisation (6).

Being poor in natural resources, Japan's effort to industrialise meant heavy dependence from the beginning on foreign markets for both exports and imports: Japan had to import modern plants and machinery and vital industrial resources like cotton. And in order to pay for them, Japan had to earn foreign exchange by exporting whatever it was able to produce. Yet the Japanese were totally unequipped with the marketing skills and facilities needed to conduct international trade. They had to rely on the services of Western traders, who opened merchant houses (called shokan) in the major port cities. Japanese traders contacted these merchant houses in order to sell their products and to purchase the foreign goods Japan needed at home. No wonder, then, that "Western merchants and the Chinese assistants fully exploited the relative naivety and ignorance of Japanese traders" (7).

With the help of the government and above all by dint of their own ingenuity, large Japanese trading companies soon began to short-circuit foreign traders and to engage directly in exporting and importing activities. With amazing speed they set up a network of overseas offices and acquired the necessary trading skills through trial and error. As a consequence, the proportion of Japanese exports handled by foreign traders dropped from as high as 86 per cent in 1880 to less than 50 per cent by 1911. Similarly, the ratio of Japanese imports handled by foreign merchants declined from 97 per cent to 36 per cent (8). This development was no doubt a successful case of import substitution in commerce, a gradual substitution of foreign expertise by indigenous skills in international transactions.

Thus Japan's exports and imports eventually came to be intermediated by its own trading companies, and the omnipresence of general trading companies in Japan's international trade became a distinctive feature. They were fostered as the leading edge of Japan's nationalism, to replace "imperialistic" Western merchants. Mitsui Busan (now Mitsui & Co.) and Mitsubishi Shoji (now Mitsubishi Corporation) expanded as the commercial wings of their respective zaibatsu groups with secure sources of income derivable from shoken -- "commercial rights" or "rights to intermediate transactions" (9).

POSTWAR REORGANISATION AND GROWTH

Given the fact that the trading company, in close collaboration with its affiliated zaibatsu group, served as an instrument of nationalistic interest supporting Japan's militarism during World War II, it was little wonder that the Allied Occupation Authorities under the command of General MacArthur concluded that the zaibatsu groups and their trading companies were impediments to a democratic free-market economy. The Occupation Authorities quickly ordered their dissolution as an essential part of the sweeping democratisation of Japan's social system. The Mitsui trading company was forced to splinter into 170 specialised small trading firms, with the former managers of departments or branches of the dissolved firms as organisers and top executives. Mitsubishi Shoji was broken up into 139 small companies.

It was during this period that five Osaka-based textile traders, who were left untouched by the dissolution order because of their relatively small-scale operations, began to quickly transform themselves into general trading companies by moving into trading in metals, metal products and machinery. Indeed they soon overtook the former zaibatsu trading companies as leaders in the field.

But this did not last long. A favourable turn of events was imminent for the dismantled zaibatsu groups. The deepening cold war between the United States and the Soviet Union and the Communist take-over of mainland China made the American Occupation Authorities more concerned with a quick economic recovery than with the idealistic reform initially contemplated. They now wanted to make Japan a capitalistic bulwark against communism. It is also said that American business interests became deeply suspicious and critical of the trust-busting zeal shown by the Occupation Authorities and feared similar developments in the United States. Some conservative American politicians sided with the business interests. Finally, the Deconcentration Review Board was dispatched from the United States in 1948, and the zaibatsu dissolution programme was virtually halted in August 1949.

Then the Korean war broke out. With this political turnabout, reunification of the zaibatsu was implicitly encouraged by the Occupation Authorities as a means of mobilising Japan's industrial resources to meet the supply needs of the Allies in Korea. The Japanese quickly moved to reconstruct the zaibatsu groups. As soon as Japan regained political autonomy in 1951, the Japanese Government amended the American-designed Anti-Monopoly Act of 1947 so as to permit intercorporate stockholding and interlocking directorates, with the ambiguous proviso that competition not be substantially restrained. It did not, however, legalise the return of holding companies. The industrial groups that subsequently emerged were, therefore, different from the feudalistic zaibatsu. There was much more vigorous competition among groups, and each component firm remained essentially autonomous, while participating in the group's overall policy formulation and co-ordination efforts.

Indeed, the initial measures taken by the American authorities to break up the zaibatsu eradicated the feudalistic remnants of Japan's economic structure but left a high degree of industrial concentration untouched. This was an ideal situation for Japan to reorganise its postwar industrial structure more effectively in a concentrated form. It was against the backdrop of this zaibatsu rehabilitation that Mitsui & Co. and Mitsubishi Corporation regained their former predominant position in short order.

Mitsubishi's restoration proceeded in two significant steps. The first wave of mergers to reunite formerly splintered units occurred in 1952, when the use of the original zaibatsu name was no longer prohibited. For example, Kowa Jitsugyo, one of Mitsubishi Shoji's central units, changed its name back to Mitsubishi Shoji in August 1952. By then Mitsubishi's splintered units had already been regrouped into four trading companies -- Mitsubishi Shoji, Fuji Shoji, Tokyo Boeki, and Tozai Boeki. And it was only a matter of time before they merged into one company. Two years later, after careful negotiations and with the blessing of Japan's Fair Trade Commission, they finally agreed on a grand merger in July 1954, an agreement that marked the second stage of reintegration (10).

Mitsubishi's success provided a strong incentive for the Mitsui group. Since Mitsui had been broken up into many more independent units than Mitsubishi, its restoration took more time, and it was not until February 1959 that the two major Mitsui trading companies' tributaries, Mitsui Bussan and Dai-Ichi Bussan, each of which had by then successfully re-absorbed many splintered units, reached a final merger agreement (11).

It is worth emphasizing that the re-emergence of Japan's powerful trading companies proceeded pari passu with the restoration of the former zaibatsu groups, as well as with the creation of new industrial groups, each of them patronising at least one general trading company as its sales and procurement agent. Indeed, the success of Sumitomo Shoji (now Sumitomo Corporation) as a brand-new trading company in the postwar period would not have been possible if it had not been backed up by the Sumitomo zaibatsu, a group consisting of large companies in such industries as heavy machinery, chemicals, metals, banking, insurance and real estate.

Now that the holding companies and zaibatsu family councils are fading memories, how do the industrial groups achieve co-ordination among their independent member companies? This task is accomplished largely by a club consisting of a selected number of elite enterprises in each group and various ad hoc committees comprised of member companies. The Mitsubishi group, for example, operates the Friday Club, represented by the presidents and chairmen of 28 key enterprises from its 50 leading companies. And Mitsubishi Corporation often plays the pivotal role of spokesman for the group.

The ties of the general trading companies to their respective industrial groups can be summarised as follows. Mitsubishi Corporation: the Mitsubishi group (the Friday Club, 28 companies); Mitsui & Co.: the Mitsui group (the Nimoku Club, 23 companies); Sumitomo Corporation: the Sumitomo group (the Hakusui Club, 21 companies); Marubeni Corporation: the Fuyo group (the Fuyo Club, 29 companies); C. Itoh & Co. and Kanematsu Gosho: the Dai-Ichi Kangyo group (the Sankin Club, 45 companies); Nissho-Iwai and Nichimen Jitsugyo: the Sanwa group (the Sansui Club, 36 companies); Tomen: the Tokai group (the Satsuki Club, five companies).

The number of companies given for each group includes only the leading companies, which constitute the apex. Each group is shaped like a pyramid, with a broad base that is comprised of countless small subcontracting firms. In fact, each group has practically an entire spectrum of industries. It can indeed be considered "a mini-economy". These six groups alone account for about one-quarter of the total assets, paid-in capital and sales of all Japanese business corporations.

THE PUSH FOR MULTINATIONAL INTERMEDIATION

Japan's swift industrialisation in the postwar period increased its dependence on overseas resources at an enormous pace. Japan soon became the world's leading importer of many key primary commodities. As a consequence, trading companies' intermediation role in imports naturally increased. At the same time, the "export-or perish" policy pursued by the Japanese Government created additional business opportunities and gave them a respectable image as the trail-blazers of Japan's export drive.

From 1965 to 1974, during the super-growth period of the Japanese economy, for example, the total value of transactions by the Top Nine trading companies increased at an annual rate of 24 per cent, which was much higher than the 17 per cent growth rate of nominal GNP (12). It also reached an unprecedented high percentage of GNP -- 32 per cent -- in 1974. Indeed, the year 1974 marked the trading companies' zenith. After that, the total value of their transactions began to peak out and even declined slightly, despite the continuous, though slower, growth of the Japanese economy. The ratio of their total sales to GNP continued to decline and dipped below 20 per cent in 1978 (see figure "Transaction Value of the Top Nine Traders" on following page).

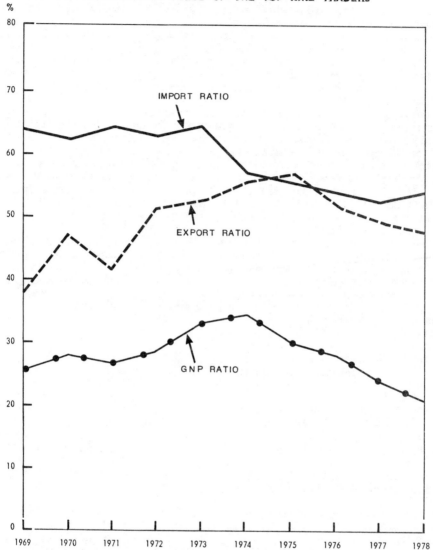

TRANSACTION VALUE OF THE TOP NINE TRADERS

IMPORT RATIO

EXPORT RATIO

GNP RATIO

Source : Adapted from Kyoikusha, *Sogo Shosha no Keiei Hikaku* (Comparison of General Trading Companies' Management) Kyoikusha, Tokyo, 1980, p. 18.

The traders' weakening position in the Japanese economy is also reflected in a slight decline of their profit margins, a trend that emerged after the Arab oil crisis of 1973 (see Annex 2, Table 1). However, even before the oil crisis, their profit margins had been extremely narrow by any business standards, running at between only 2 to 3 per cent. On the average, as much as $1 million in sales still brings only $20 000 in profits. The only way to make up for such a thin profit margin is to engage in as large a volume of transactions as possible.

The slowdown of the Japanese economy since 1973 has been responsible for a decline in the growth of traders' intermediation business as well as increasingly fierce competition for bigger shares of the market. Losses sustained as a result of unexpected drops in the prices of such commodities as sugar and copper, a sharp appreciation of the Japanese yen in 1978 and the second oil crisis of 1979 dealt further blows to the trading companies.

In addition to these unforeseen developments that weakened the relative position of the traders, longer-term forces had been at work. Many years earlier some people had predicted that the role of the general trading companies as marketing intermediaries would inevitably decline. In 1961 the so-called "demise thesis" was advanced in a popular business journal (13). In essence it was argued that, as manufacturers developed and accumulated marketing skills for their own differentiated products (which also necessitated company- and product-specific after-sales services), their reliance on general trading companies would necessarily be reduced. Yet the business of trading companies continued to thrive throughout the 1960s as the Japanese economy advanced by leaps and bounds. Although many manufacturers with established brand names -- and particularly those of differentiated consumer durables -- did succeed in setting up their own exporting channels, ample opportunities to intermediate business transactions still remained -- and in fact expanded -- for trading companies, particularly in the area of procuring raw industrial materials and energy resources from overseas.

Even so, the 1970s brought in an entirely different environment. Because of fundamental structural changes in the Japanese economy, the trading companies were quickly losing their raison d'être. First, with the maturing of the economy, the tertiary (or service) sector was expanding at a much faster rate than the primary and secondary sectors. Although commerce itself belongs to the tertiary sector, trading companies were unable to "intermediate" in such service-related activities as restaurants and leisure businesses unless they became directly engaged in such activities themselves. Some companies did move in this direction -- Mitsubishi tied up with Kentucky Fried Chicken and Mitsui entered a joint venture with the U.S. company Brunswick in a bowling-alley operation -- but efforts clearly lagged behind the overall trend.

Second, the three major items trading companies had been handling -- steel, chemicals, and textiles, which alone accounted for more than half their business -- were the very industries whose sales, both at home and overseas, now grew only at a much slower pace than before. At the same time, Japan's top exports shifted away from these traditional specialities of the trading companies to such new export items as electronic products, automobiles and precision machinery, goods that do not require much export assistance from trading companies.

Thirdly, the quasi-banking function of general trading companies (a function to be detailed in the following section) lost some of its importance as many manufacturers began to accumulate their own internal funds.

Given these developments, which eroded their business base at home, trading companies began to look beyond their domestic markets and expanded their overseas operations to seek out new business territories. Their efforts toward multinationalism will be examined in Chapter III.

THE QUASI-BANKERS

Japan's major trading companies are certainly more than simple commission brokers acting as go-betweens. According to Peter F. Drucker, "In many ways, the trading company is not a 'trading company', but a 'finance company'" (14). In his view, the banking role of trading companies can be traced to the fact that, following the Meiji Restoration in 1868, the government gave distribution much lower priority than production in the early stages of industrialisation and medium-term money markets remained underdeveloped.

"A trading company" he writes, "is the one way in which the Japanese company manages its medium-term credit problem, for the trading company optimizes the need for medium-term credit. The trading company creates its own money pool, or what bankers call a 'float' -- a reservoir of money that can be used whenever the need arises and that can be turned over a great deal faster than money invested in any one distribution channel or cycle. It creates a medium-term money market, and does so very effectively. ... It represents the most rational optimization of the existing structures, under which medium-term finance is critically short and inadequately taken care of by the existing banking system. ... Just as the zaibatsu bank is the capital market of Japan, so the trading company is its money market."

Nowadays, in fact, the trading company supplies not only short- to medium-term loans in connection with its trade-intermediating activities but also equity capital to foster its own suppliers. Such equity capital ranges from a relatively small 32 per cent (for Kanematsu Gosho) to as much as 64 per cent (for Sumitomo Corporation) of its total financing activity (see Annex 2, Table 2). This equity-debt financing ratio has been on the rise throughout the postwar period as the trading companies have tried to solidify their position as financiers, marketing agents and overseas investment organisers for their respective industrial groups.

With the exception of Mitsubishi Corporation, which enjoys a comparatively high rate of return (9.4 per cent) on its investment -- mostly from its very lucrative investment in Brunei natural gas -- trading companies earn only a very low rate of return, ranging from 1.2 to 3.1 per cent, hardly an attractive rate by any investment standard. They are, on the other hand, a crucial conduit for trading activities. In fact, so long as an investment project leads to intermediating activities that generate commissions, trading companies have apparently been content to accept a low rate of return on the investment itself. They are now actively investing overseas, and their overseas finance accounts for from anywhere between 20 per cent (for C. Itoh) to 42 per cent (for Marubeni and Tomen).

In short, as financial institutions, Japan's general trading companies are unique. They combine the roles of the British merchant bank, which was founded to provide medium-term loans for foreign trade, and the German universal bank, which is heavily committed to financing its affiliated industrial group. But the important difference is that Japan's trading companies are quite willing to accept an extremely low rate of return on financial investment in exchange for other business transactions that enable them to earn commissions. The financing services of a trading company may perhaps be likened to what in marketing jargon is called a "loss leader", which is used to attract customers to other items the store sells.

THE INFORMATION-GATHERERS

Each trading company has spun a vast web of information-gathering. Its capacity to collect not only economic but also social and political information is said to be far superior to that of the Japanese Government, as far as both geographical and topical coverage is concerned. The hub of the trading company's intelligence service is the home office in Japan. Each home office is the "debriefing" point for company employees returning from overseas, as well as the centre of a telex network. Information flowing in through the telex system is handled by a specially-trained communication corps.

Mitsui & Co., for example, is said to have the most comprehensive, sophisticated system, called a "global on-line network system"; telex-cum-computers are strategically installed in five key cities around the world. The daily volume of telex communication can amount to as many as 80 000 dispatches and receipts, a volume far larger than that handled by any other trading company. In 1978, Mitsui spent 11 936 million yen (15) for communications alone -- telex, telephone, facsimile, postage and computer time -- an amount equivalent to one-third of the company's total payroll.

Other trading companies, too, invest large sums of money in communications (see Annex 2, Table 3). Communications expenses as a proportion of sales expenditure for the Top Nine range from 1.9 per cent (for Tomen) to as high as 9.6 per cent (for Mitsui). Apart from these extremes, which are actually not strictly comparable, the normal range for the other seven companies is somewhere between 3 and 5 per cent. This ratio can perhaps be compared in importance to that of research and development (R&D) expenditure to sales for manufacturers. And indeed, it does roughly correspond in size to the average research and development-to-sales ratio in such technology-intensive manufacturing industries as electronics (3.9 per cent).

The heavy communications expenses incurred by trading companies are thus a form of corporate investment, similar to that in R&D. But unlike R&D-oriented manufacturers, they generate little knowledge of their own. Trading companies have a comparative advantage not in generating but in collecting and disseminating information. As will be discussed in Annex 1, this characteristic has an important theoretical implication for the behaviour of trading companies as multinationals.

In addition to the information that is gathered through regular intra-firm communication channels and stored in files or computers, trading companies also accumulate what may be called "human-embodied knowledge" in the form of individual employees' expertise. Hence, as could be expected, labour costs are the largest component (50 to 60 per cent) of the trading companies' total operating costs.

The rate of return on investment in information-gathering (intelligence activities) in advanced countries is probably much higher than that in developing countries because of the ease of communications and transportation and the availability of information in the form of publications, broadcasting, lectures, public meetings and so forth. No wonder, then, that the heavy concentration of Japan's manufacturing and extractive investment in developing countries (about 70 per cent) contrasts sharply with the relatively small commerce-related investment (33 per cent) located in those countries. In fact, information about developing countries itself can often be collected more effectively in key political centres in advanced countries. Subsequent to the fall of the Shah of Iran, for example, all the major trading companies established liaison offices in Washington, D.C.

ORGANISERS/CO-ORDINATORS

General trading companies have recently developed another role, that of organiser/co-ordinator. After some groping, they have succeeded in setting up this new business function very effectively to meet the challenges of a new economic environment. It is a reflection of their adaptability, experience and acumen. Initially experimented at home in the 1960s, the organiser/co-ordinator function is now actively applied to trading companies' overseas ventures, as they have gained experience and confidence through "learning-by-doing".

This organiser/co-ordinator role developed out of a synergic combination of the trading companies' major traditional functions which we examined earlier: transaction intermediation, quasi-banking and information-gathering. It may be broken down into two types: a "converter" (or "downstream operator") type, and a "developer" (or "upstream operator") type.

The converter function has come into being as a result of trading companies' efforts to cultivate consumer markets on their own by engaging in material procurement, product design and marketing as a vertically-integrated operation that moves down-stream through different stages of production. This effort represents the traders' eagerness to expand their sphere of operation, which was traditionally confined to producers' goods in the upstream stages. The trading company secures necessary raw materials or intermediate inputs and organises a production team by tying up with a manufacturer who will be in charge of producing the newly designed products specified by the trading company. Usually, the manufacturer is a small- or medium-sized company which, because it has not yet developed its own market, is willing to become a "captive supplier" or a "production division" of the trading company. If the manufacturer's production skill is inadequate, the trading company brings in the necessary technology from the outside under a licensing agreement.

This converter formula has proved successful most notably in the apparel industry. For example, Mitsui & Co. markets through its affiliated retail outlets the suits, trousers, shirts and neckties manufactured in collaboration with Daitobo Co., with the use of know-how imported from Friedman-Marks Co. of the United States. Mitsubishi Corporation has a Korean firm manufacture dress shirts, with technology licensed by the Takahara Shirt Manufacturing Co. of Japan (16).

Restaurants and fast-food chains are another important consumer market in which trading companies have shown interest. Mitsubishi Corporation, for instance, operates what has become an unexpectedly successful chain of instant-noodle restaurants called "Larmen Dosanko" in New York. They ultimately aim to open 100 stores throughout the United States.

This franchising business started in 1975 but, five years previously, Mitsubishi had become the Japanese partner of the Kentucky Fried Chicken operation. It is perhaps no coincidence that Mitsubishi moved to take up the instant-noodle franchising on its own after its experience with Kentucky Fried Chicken. Although restaurant franchising does not involve much vertically-integrated operation, it does demonstrate the trader's effort to move downstream and capture consumer markets. Trading companies have indeed come a long way from the days when they earned commissions on cotton, rice, steel, machinery and other upstream commodities.

Their latest move in this connection has been to advance into more technology-based sectors, such as personal computers and computer peripherals. For example, C. Itoh & Co. is currently marketing overseas, under its own house brand, small printers produced by a manufacturer which it has successfully supported as a subsidiary.

Because of the wide range of their trading activities, trading companies are in a position to span different segments of a market, both vertically and horizontally. The more fluid (hence the more competitive) the market, the easier it is for trading companies to enter it and profit from their converter function. With rising personal incomes, consumers' tastes tend to become more diversified. Trading companies are now aggressively trying to orient themselves towards these growing consumer markets, which are highly inconstant and hence, in their view, "up for grabs".

The "developer" or "upstream operator" type of the organiser/co-ordinator function originated at home when the general trading companies began to become involved in developing, in collaboration with other companies affiliated with a particular industrial group, such industrial complexes as petrochemical and food kombinatos, as they were called in Japan. From the mid-1950s to the early 1960s, major petrochemical kombinatos were constructed one after another. The Mitsui group was the first to build an integrated petrochemical complex at Iwakuni, the plant being owned by Mitsui Petrochemical. Mitsui & Co. naturally became the exclusive distributor of petrochemicals produced at the plant. Similarly, Mitsubishi Petrochemical Co. established the Mitsubishi group's kombinato at Yokkaichi, while Sumitomo Chemical Co. set up a complex for the Sumitomo group at Niihama. Mitsubishi Corporation and Sumitomo Corporation both played a crucial role in setting up and running their industrial groups' petrochemical complexes.

The leader in food kombinatos was Tomen, which established the first of its kind in Kobe in 1967. It involved the installation of a 67 000 ton grain elevator, then Japan's largest, and a berth to accommodate a 50 000 ton

freighter, as well as the participation of a number of manufacturers to produce at the new port site such products as vegetable oil, feeds and corn-
starch (17). This stimulated the interest of other trading companies.
Mitsui & Co., for example, quickly set up similar food kombinatos in a few
cities. All were designed to generate -- and at the same time, capture --
external economies or economically favourable operational links among the
participants. The kombinato resulted in increased efficiency and a substantial reduction in both production and distribution costs.

APPLYING NEW-FOUND SKILLS IN THIRD WORLD COUNTRIES

Having learned from these successful domestic operations, general trading companies were soon applying their newly acquired systems-focussed skills
abroad, and particularly in Third World countries, where such developer skills
were in both short supply and great demand for industrialisation efforts. For
example, at the end of the 1960s, Mitsubishi Corporation hit upon the idea of
building an international airport at Mombasa, Kenya, to exploit promising
tourist resources for regional development. A feasibility study begun in 1970
was enthusiastically received by the Kenyan Government which, however, was unable to finance the project. Mitsubishi then lobbied for a special yen loan
from the Japanese Government. Though no such loan had ever been offered before to an African country, the Japanese Government, after some hesitation,
was finally persuaded to extend it as economic assistance. (As will be seen
in Chapter V, many of Japan's large-scale economic-assistance projects were
initiated by private firms.) It took Mitsubishi over three years to secure
the necessary funding and another five years to complete the airport. The
company used its organiser/co-ordinator capacity to arrange and supervise all
the construction work; it hired builders and procured materials and equipment. Upon completion, the airport quickly attracted such international carriers as Lufthansa, BOAC, Alitalia and Finnair, which now bring in a large
number of tourists. Hotels and other tourist-related facilities have been
constructed as the forward linkage of the airport, stimulating regional economic growth.

Following the success of the Mombasa project, Mitsubishi Corporation
was asked by Malawi, Kenya's southern neighbour, to construct a similar airport. The company again secured special loans from both the Japanese Government and the African Development Bank and began construction of an airport in
1978. With these experiences behind it, Mitsubishi Corporation, along with
Shimizu Construction Co. of Japan, bid successfully in 1979 for a large urban
renewal project in Baghdad, Iraq, a project calling for construction of 34
high-rise residential buildings, a town hall, schools, and office and shopping
centres (18).

These moves to become project organisers were aptly pinpointed in one
company's recent advertisement: "If Rome had to be built in a day,
Nissho-Iwai would most likely get the job: Nissho-Iwai is a project organiser
in resource and industrial development. We build urban infrastructures. Introduce joint venture partners. Invest in national growth. Finance. Inform
and advise."

General trading companies do not produce any physical goods themselves but specialise in intermediating between buyers and sellers of goods. Space and time are the two dimensions in which they operate, and they profit from the movement of goods and services. Although they perform many functions, trade intermediation is their major source of income. In 1978, for example, the Top Nine trading companies as a group earned 62.7 per cent of their income from trade intermediation, 27.8 per cent from quasi-banking, and 5.6 per cent in the form of dividends from investments (19).

In intermediating trade, they play two roles, broker and speculator. As brokers, traders do not acquire the ownership of goods to be transacted; they simply assist their clients on a commission basis in finding buyers or sellers, as the case may be. In this role, their activity always contributes to social welfare without creating a divergence between private and social benefits. On the other hand, traders in their capacity of speculators aggressively acquire the ownership, albeit temporarily, of goods in the hope of selling them at higher prices. Although this type of buying and selling may help producers clear their unwanted inventories (that is, transfer their inventory function to traders) and stabilise prices (if they buy low and sell high), it can often end up in market-cornering activities that adversely affect consumers' welfare. This dual characteristic of trade intermediation should be kept in mind when evaluating the welfare implications of trading companies' operations.

Given the particular types of specialised services they offer, the trading companies perform functions that are highly complementary to the needs of both producers and buyers who lack capacities in marketing (especially exporting and importing), financing, warehousing, transportation and investing overseas, that is, generally speaking, small-scale companies. Indeed, trading companies can turn these small-scale manufacturers into multinationals by supplementing all their requirements.

According to Louis Wolf Goodman, "The MNC [Multinational Corporation] activity most frequently discussed in the social scientific literature is direct foreign investment (DFI). However, DFI is only one of a number of business activities carried out by MNCs. In fact, it is more sensible to think of DFI as an integrated package of the range of business operations available to firms.

"These operations include importing and exporting raw materials and goods in various stages of manufacture; licensing agreements which authorize the use of patented technologies and trademarks; management contracts, which provide managerial services and 'knowhow' for a fee; service contracts, which provide for the maintenance and upgrading of plants, equipment, and processes; equity investment, entitling the investor to a share of dividends; capital lending, wherein the MNC loans funds to the firms in the nation; marketing contracts, where products of a country are sold in international markets by an MNC; and even financial speculation, where the operations of a corporation in a Third World nation allow the MNC to attempt to take advantage of fluctuations in international money markets" (20).

This characterisation of MNC activity does point up the significance of firm size, for only large corporations can afford to possess such an "integrated package" of key business operations. In the terminology of Kenneth Galbraith, technostructure is considered essential for a given corporation to go multinational successfully on its own. Yet, interestingly enough, trading companies can give pre-technostructural firms an opportunity to go overseas as multinationals, since the former are in a position to offer the corporate resources that are lacking. The existence of such unique general trading companies in Japan thus led to the equally unique phenomenon of a large number of overseas investments made by small- and medium-sized firms, especially in developing countries (more on this in Chapter IV).

In addition to assisting small-scale manufacturers in setting up overseas operations, trading companies are now more active than ever in supplying the same services to large-scale regional development ventures abroad, notably resource-related ventures in the Third World, a role that has clearly grown more important since the 1973 oil crisis.

Chapter III

INVESTMENTS IN TRADING NETWORKS ABROAD

In the early postwar period, Japan's general trading companies gradually re-established their trading networks in major commercial centres abroad. Although Japan was then short of foreign exchange reserves, the government placed a high priority on the restoration of the trading companies' global networks in order to encourage exports and secure vital supplies of key industrial resources. The companies were given special consideration for exchange allocations.

New York, London, Paris, Dusseldorf, Sydney, Sao Paulo, Hong Kong and Bangkok were among the major cities to which trading companies went back to set up branches and local offices in order to re-establish their pre-war business connections (see Annex 2, Table 4a). These outposts were for a while limited in scale of operation but grew quite rapidly with the swift recovery and expansion of the Japanese economy and its overseas trade. Many were soon transformed from mere offices of representatives to branches, and from branches to locally incorporated subsidiaries.

At the same time, trading companies' networks expanded in geographical coverage, embracing many more cities throughout the world. In particular relatively big offices with a large number of employees were set up in the developed regions -- North America, Europe, and Oceania -- which were of special commercial interest and significance for the trading companies. For example, Mitsui's New York subsidiary, Mitsui & Co. (U.S.A.), is now the largest of the trading companies' wholly-owned overseas subsidiaries with well over 600 people.

By and large, the larger the trading company (that is, in terms of total sales), the more extensive its geographical coverage by way of key overseas subsidiaries. Obviously there is a reinforcing causality between sales and scale of operation overseas: the more active a trading company is in its overseas transactions, the larger the number of its overseas subsidiaries, and vice versa. Their ranking as multinationals closely reflects the size of their total sales, both at home and abroad. In other words, for trading companies, degree of multinationalisation is a function of firm size.

It is worth noting that although all the nine trading companies have either a branch office or a representative in London, with the exception of Mitsui & Co., they have not transformed those outposts into locally incorporated regional headquarters. For example, Sumitomo Corporation has regional headquarters in Rotterdam, Paris, Milan, Brussels, Dusseldorf and Athens, but has none in London. This is partly because Britain delayed entering the European Economic Community (EEC), and as the trading companies were attracted to the EEC, they decided to focus on Continental Europe. Paris, Dusseldorf and Brussels, in particular, were chosen as strategic locations for their European business operations. The only exception is Mitsui & Co., Europe Ltd. (London), which serves as Mitsui's European headquarters. Nissho-Iwai's London branch office serves as the central office for European operations but it is not locally incorporated.

However, with Britain's entry into the EEC and the growth of the Euro-currency market, London has become just as important. All the trading companies' London offices, whether locally incorporated or not, are now no doubt playing an increasingly important role, especially in financial activities.

One may wonder why all these traders' overseas headquarters are located in the same countries and, in fact, practically in the same cities. It is natural that, as traders, they should congregate in the world's major commercial centres. It is not surprising, for example, that each has its largest foreign subsidiary in New York. Yet their presence in many of the same localities also reflects the high degree of oligopolistic rivalry that exists among them. When one trading company, especially a leading one, sets up a subsidiary, a branch office or even a small representative office in a new location overseas, the move is closely watched and often imitated -- the familiar "bandwagon" type of behaviour observable in any oligopolistic competition.

Yet when it comes to overseas transactions, where trading companies are often confronted with a common competitive threat or want to reach the same objectives, they forego their fierce rivalry and join forces. Even information is actively shared for mutual benefit, so long as it is not directly commercial and proprietary. In fact, companies go so far as to form joint ventures abroad. This need to collaborate no doubt induces trading companies to cluster together in a given location overseas.

Another question one asks oneself is why these regional offices have to be incorporated locally as "indigenous business entities" (instead of being mere branch offices or representative offices) and wholly-owned (instead of being majority-owned). Clearly, local incorporation implies setting up an "indigenous" firm and entails many advantages (and obligations) unavailable to a foreign firm. Tax advantages are one example: in the United States, "indigenous" firms can set up Domestic International Sales Corporations (DISCs) to enjoy a special tax exemption from export earnings. To be eligible for bidding for local government business, indigenisation is likewise required.

Wholly-owned operations are also a necessity, for this is the surest way for trading companies to control their commercial information as exclusively as possible. As discussed in Chapter II, information-gathering is a form of investment, and trading companies strive to enhance the appropriability of benefits from such investment through wholly-owned operations. But, as commission brokers, they have to work closely with other business firms and cannot always keep their business partners in commercial overseas ventures in the dark, no matter how much they may want to keep their information exclusive.

To escape from this dilemma they have come up with an innovative system of organisation by setting up separate ventures with other companies whose interests must be accommodated as joint investors. Trading companies have also found it both necessary and desirable to organise separately from their regional headquarters a string of small wholly-owned trading units that specialise in particular lines of trading. These can be called "auxiliary trading ventures" and should be distinguished from the trading companies' key regional offices.

There are several variations of auxiliary set-ups, which can be classified into eight types.

We shall refer to this classification in the rest of the study.

A CLASSIFICATION OF AUXILIARY TRADING VENTURES

Type A : Ventures wholly-owned by the home office of a trading company.

Type A': Ventures wholly-owned by a regional office of a trading company

Type B : Joint ventures owned by the home office of a trading company and a Japanese company (or companies). These ventures are still fully controlled by Japanese interests.

Type B': Joint ventures owned by a regional office of a trading company and a Japanese company (or companies). These ventures are still fully controlled by Japanese interests.

Type C : Joint ventures between the home office of a trading company and local interests

Type C': Joint ventures between a regional office of a trading company and local interests

Type D : Joint ventures among the home office of a trading company, a Japanese company (or companies) and local interests (and/or third country interests)

Type D': Joint ventures among a regional office of a trading company, a Japanese company (or companies) and local interests (and/or third country interests).

These various types of ventures deserve further explanation.

Type A: The home office sets up a wholly-owned overseas subsidiary to specialise in a particular line of trading -- for example, in cotton, grain, oil or standardized manufactures -- which, for geographical, financial or any other reason, requires a separate organisation. This type of venture is engaged in either procuring and shipping local products to Japan or marketing locally Japanese products whose sales do not require the direct participation of Japanese manufacturers.

Here are some examples of Type A trading ventures:

-- Marubeni owns Importadora Datsun in Chile, an import distributor of Datsun cars from Japan, with a paid-in capital of 36.54 million pesos and 90 employees.

-- Sumitomo Corporation owns Plaza Motors in Puerto Rico. It distributes Mazda motor cars and car parts, has a paid-in capital of $100 000 and employs 23 people.

-- Tomen operates Tomen Petroleum Co. in Bermuda, a trader in oil, with a paid-in capital of $136 000; it employs three people.

Type B: The home office and the Japanese manufacturer collaborate to set up a sales and customer-service company abroad to import and market that manufacturer's products exclusively. This arrangement represents an effort on the part of trading companies to hold on to the lucrative intermediation transactions involving brand-name products. In other words, by establishing manufacturer-specific sales ventures, trading companies are trying to prevent the so-called "departure-from-traders" trend, a phenomenon discussed in Chapter II. These ventures are designed to promote the export of manufactured products from Japan.

In most cases, the manufacturers are majority-interest holders (50 to 70 per cent), and trading companies are allowed to retain their shoken (commercial rights) to deal exclusively with the manufacturers' products as a joint investor in overseas sales networks:

-- Casio Computer Co. GmbH. in West Germany is a joint venture between Tomen (40 per cent interest) and Casio (60 per cent interest) to sell Casio's electronics products, with a paid-in capital of DM3 million and 37 employees.

-- Mazda Motors of Benelux in Belgium is owned by Toyo Kogyo (70 per cent interest) and Sumitomo (30 per cent interest) with a paid-in capital of BF5 million and 68 employees to distribute Mazda auto parts.

All Type B ventures with only one exception are located in advanced countries.

Type C: In this set-up the home office chooses local interests as investment partners. No third party is involved. Transactions in this type of bilateral venture involve manufactures or local primary products, such as tobacco or grain. The former are imported from Japan and sold to local markets, while the latter are exported mostly to Japan. These ventures are usually designed to take advantage of the commercial skills possessed by local merchants.

-- Inter-Asian Tobacco Exporters Co., Thailand, is a joint venture between Mitsui & Co. (29.4 per cent interest) and local interests (70.6 per cent interest), engaged in exporting tobacco leaves from Thailand. It is capitalised at 4 million bahts and employs 848 people.

-- Formac S.A., Brazil, is a joint venture between C. Itoh & Co. (24.5 per cent interest) and local interests (75.5 per cent interest), a sales company for construction machinery. It is capitalised at CR25.4 million and employs 110 people.

-- Nichimen do Mexico S.A., Mexico, is a joint venture between Nichimen (75 per cent interest) and local interests (25 per cent interest), engaged in exporting agricultural products. It is capitalised at 7.5 million pesos.

Type D: This category represents tripartite joint ventures involving the home office, other Japanese companies (mostly manufacturers but occasionally other trading companies), and local interests. It is the most frequently used of the different variations.

-- Sapporo Beer, Ltd., Hong Kong, is a tripartite joint venture among Sapporo Beer Co. of Japan (76 per cent interest), Mitsui & Co. (20 per cent interest), and local interests (4 per cent interest), a venture to market the beer and foods produced by Sapporo Beer. It is capitalised at HK\$300 000 and employs 20 people.

-- D. Worachak International Co., Thailand, is a joint venture among Mitsubishi Corporation (18 per cent interest), Mitsubishi Electric Co. (40 per cent interest), and local interests (42 per cent interest), to market, install, and service elevators and air-conditioners. It is capitalised at 3 million bahts and employs 63 people.

The four other types -- A', B', C', and D' -- are identical with Types A, B, C and D, respectively, except that the overseas investments are made by a trading company's key regional offices instead of by the home office.

Why, then, do the trading companies' regional offices themselves have to become investors? That is, why doesn't the home office alone take care of all overseas investments? There are many conceivable reasons for the emergence of "grandson" ventures. For one thing, such a development shows the maturing process of key regional offices. These subsidiaries are growing into fully-fledged "local" general trading companies in the image of the parent companies and are spinning a web of their own satellite companies, albeit still on a small scale, just as their parent companies do both at home and abroad. In this sense, they are no longer mere regional offices (or branch subsidiaries) but are becoming "independent" companies in their own right. Indeed, this particular process of localisation of regional offices is actually encouraged by the home offices.

Moreover, overseas ventures established by regional offices (which are locally incorporated "indigenised" companies) can create a more favourable image than those set up by the home office of a purely foreign company. From the point of view of public relations, indigenised companies can be seen as ventures set up and controlled by "immigrants who are committed to becoming local citizens." The fact that regional offices set up third-generation ventures can be interpreted as a sign of their eagerness to plow back profits into the local economies. In addition to this public-relations benefit, investments in a network of third-generation ventures give regional offices an opportunity to diversify financial risks and to expand their network of commercial information. As is the case with the parent companies, the holding of satellite companies also leads to new business opportunities for inter-mediating diversified trade transactions.

In 1980 there were a total of 245 auxiliary ventures set up by the nine trading companies. As might be expected, the larger a trading company, the greater the number of such investments. The four largest companies -- Mitsui Mitsubishi, Marubeni, and C. Itoh -- alone account for more than 70 per cent of these auxiliary trading ventures. In general, the home offices are more active in creating Type D tripartite joint ventures than any other type, whereas the regional offices are the least active in establishing Type D ventures. The most frequent form of auxilairy ventures adopted by regional offices is joint ventures with other Japanese companies (Type B').

As far as regional distribution is concerned, home offices opt most often to set up Type A and B ventures in North America, while Types B and C are the most popular in Europe, and Type D is the dominant form in Oceania. Types A and C are relatively frequent in Latin America, while Types C and D are predominant in Asia. Thus there seems to be no discernible difference in the use of different types of ventures between industrialised and developing host countries. Yet one significant difference does emerge when the auxiliary ventures set up or participated in by overseas regional offices are examined. The regional offices are definitely more active in establishing their auxil-iary trading ventures in the industrialised regions than in the developing ones (see Annex 2 Table 4b)

THE COMMODITIES HANDLED BY AUXILIARY TRADING VENTURES

When the 245 auxiliary trading ventures entered into by the Top Nine companies by 1980 are broken down by commodities, one finds that 33 (13.5 per cent) specialised in primary commodities (agricultural, marine, and forestry products, minerals and fuels). Sixteen ventures (6.5 per cent) did not spe-cialise in any particular commodity; they were "general" traders but their scale of operation was limited (see Annex 2 Table 4c).

On the other hand, 196 of the auxiliary ventures specialised in parti-cular lines of manufacture. Interestingly enough, the highest percentage (13.5 per cent) was still in motor cars, motorcycles, and parts. In the early days of Japan's drive to export motor cars and motorcycles, producers depended on the services of trading companies, but this proved so successful that pro-ducers were later able to expand their sales and service facilities indepen-dently. Today, when automobile manufacturers move into local production in new foreign markets, they seldom choose traders as joint investors. Most of the still existing tie-ups between the automobile producers and trading companies date back to the early period (that is, before the "departure-from-traders" phenomenon occurred).

Non-electric machinery (such as tractors and farm equipment), electric machinery (ranging from household electrical appliances to elevators), textiles, and metal products are also popular lines of manufacture. They account for 12.2 per cent, 10.2 per cent, and 9 per cent, respectively, of auxiliary trading ventures.

OWNERSHIP INTEREST

As joint investors, the trading companies are more often minority owners than majority owners, whether investments are made by their home office or by the regional offices (see Annex 2 Table 4d). They hold minority interests (49 per cent or less) in 142 of their 245 ventures (that is, 57.9 per cent occurrence). Yet majority ownership (80 to 100 per cent ownership) is fairly important, taking 22.5 per cent of the total.

Type A and Type A' ventures are by definition wholly-owned by the home office of a trading company and its regional offices, respectively. These 100 per cent-owned ventures, 50 of them altogether, account for about 20 per cent (50 out of 245) of the total number of auxiliary trading ventures. It should also be noted that although Type B and Type B' ventures are joint ventures, they are in fact totally owned by a combination of Japanese interests. Hence Type C, C', D, and D' ventures alone represent local interests. (Only nine of the 115 ventures of Types A, A', B, and B' are located in developing regions. Hence the auxiliary trading ventures in developing countries are much more strongly characterised by minority ownership, than one might think at first glance.)

THIRD-COUNTRY (OFFSHORE) TRADE INTERMEDIATION

The trading companies are striving to "multinationalise" their operations by capturing third-country trade opportunities, in addition to home-market-linked transactions. This is called the "departure-from-Japan" phenomenon. So far, they have succeeded in "multinationalising" their trading networks but not really their operations per se. In other words, they have set up a large number of overseas offices and ventures throughout the world, but their overseas outposts have so far been largely designed to support home-country trade. Today regional headquarters -- those that are locally incorporated as "indigenised" companies -- are particularly eager to seek third-country trade which does not involve their home markets. In this way, they can gain more autonomy from the home office and become multinational in their own right.

The values of third-country trade intermediated by the Top Nine traders and the relative importance of such trade to each company's total sales varied from year to year, but in 1978 the ratios of third-country trade to total sales for the nine companies ranged from 5 per cent (for Sumitomo) to about 17 per cent (for Tomen). In absolute value terms, Marubeni ranked first and C. Itoh second over the 1976-1978 period (see Annex 2 Table 4e).

However, a large part of these third-country trade transactions is still intermediated by the trading companies' home offices rather than by their overseas trading ventures. Depending upon the accounting procedure used by a company, the home office may be "unduly" credited with such transactions even though it is the overseas offices that are actually responsible. There is, however, no way of knowing exactly how much the home office should be given credit for third-country trade since they do work closely with overseas outposts on many occasions (21).

37

The most frequent flow of third-country trade intermediated by the trading companies is said to be the trade flow "from Asia to Asia" -- that is, from one Asian country to another -- followed by the flow from Asia to North America. This is perhaps not unexpected given the trading companies' past activities and the nature of products whose trade they usually intermediate. It was in North America and especially in Asia that the trading companies initially spun their extensive marketing networks in the early postwar period to sell Japanese manufactures, such as textiles, sundries, and relatively simple machinery. In the mid-1950s, for example, approximately half of Japan's exports went to other Asian countries and about 20 per cent to the United States and Canada. Europe, Latin America and other regions accounted for less than 10 per cent each.

As the Asian economies, and particularly Hong Kong, Singapore, South Korea, and Taiwan, subsequently began to industrialise rapidly with an accompanying expansion in intra-Asian trade, Japanese trading companies quickly moved to capture this new trade opportunity. More precisely they got into trade not only between Japan and the rest of Asia but also among other Asian countries themselves by making use of their well-established networks in the region.

They soon capitalised on another opportunity to export labour-intensive manufactures from Asia to North America. The trading companies had exported such goods from Japan but began to find it increasingly difficult to do so, as their Japanese manufacturers lost trade competitiveness because of rising wages at home. In other words, the Japanese traders shifted procurement of labour-intensive manufactures from Japan to other Asian countries. In the course of this activity, they also set up a large number of manufacturing ventures in low labour-cost countries, the majority of them in Asia, in collaboration with Japanese manufacturers as well as with local interests (a topic that will be examined in Chapter IV). All these business strategies taken by the trading companies are now resulting in a rapid rise in their third-country trade intermediation, involving trade flows both from Asia to Asia and from Asia to North America.

Other trade flows, though not as significant as yet, are in decreasing order of importance, from North America to Europe, from North America to Asia, from Asia to Europe, from Asia to the Middle East, from Asia to Latin America, from Latin America to Europe, and all other third-country trade flows. It is expected that the intermediation of North America-originated trade will grow in volume rapidly, in grains (such as wheat and corn) and mineral resources (especially, aluminium and coal), particularly in the hands of such large traders as Mitsui, Mitsubishi, Marubeni and C. Itoh.

Most recently another spur has been given to third-country trade. Some developing countries and particularly Indonesia, are now demanding counter purchase exports from trading companies; if they sell to these countries, they must also purchase from them. This requirement is perhaps most strictly enforced in the case of plant exports to Indonesia, but the trading companies have so far been co-operative in complying with such a requirement, even if they are apprehensive about its possible spread to other countries. C. Itoh and Nissho-Iwai, for example, agreed to purchase Indonesian primary products in exchange for an export contract for an oil refinery worth 270 billion yen. Sumitomo also concluded a contract to export a rolling stock plant on a counter-purchase basis. Compared with the small traders from other countries, who are narrowly specialised, Japan's trading companies are in a better position to find customers for the products they must acquire under the counter-trade system -- if not at home then in third-country markets through their global networks of marketing (22).

ASSESSMENT

Although it is true that third-country trade is a fairly important portion of trading companies' business and that they are striving to expand such trade opportunities, most of their overseas ventures in commerce, whether by regional offices or as auxiliary ventures, are still largely devoted either to the sale of "made-in-Japan" manufactures or to the procurement of local primary commodities to be shipped to Japan. In this sense, their business orientation is highly "ethnocentric"; they are designed primarily to promote their home country's trading interests. Even in the types of auxiliary ventures in which local ownership is represented, (Types C, C', D and D'), locally manufactured goods are rarely handled.

One promising exception is the auxiliary ventures set up in partnership with local commercial interests that are engaged in export-import business on a small scale. Many of these joint ventures, notably in Thailand and Indonesia, are intended to assist local business in developing general trading companies of the Japanese type. This kind of arrangement involves transfers of trading and organisational skills to local interests. Indeed, the local demand to create indigenous trading companies patterned after Japan's sogo shosha is on the rise in the less developed countries. Most recently, for example, Mitsui & Co. decided to participate as a joint investor (20 per cent interest) in the establishment of Malaysia's first general trading company, Perdama SDN. BHD.

The development of comparative advantage in production alone is not sufficient if a developing country is to benefit fully from international trade. It must also develop international marketing skills and facilities. Yet at the company level, it is not an easy task for many manufacturers, particularly small ones, to organise and manage an effective international marketing unit of their own. In this regard, trading companies can serve as a surrogate sales (or procurement) department for manufacturers that cannot afford, financially or managerially, to have their own marketing unit and that remain basically production units. A division of corporate functions between production and marketing at the microeconomic level is thus achieved to meet the macro-economic requirement of strengthening a country's trade competitiveness. This is an important lesson that the developing countries can learn -- and which some are learning quickly -- from the Japanese experience.

Chapter IV

OVERSEAS MANUFACTURING VENTURES

As emphasized in Chapter II, the general trading companies play the role of organiser of manufacturing ventures; with a few exceptions, they themselves are neither much interested in nor capable of manufacturing per se. Their real interest lies in the commercial activities that are created at three different levels in the course of setting up and managing a manufacturing venture: procurement of plants, capital equipment, and machinery; supply of raw materials and intermediate products; and marketing of the output of such manufacturing ventures. Moreover, the trading companies are engaged in quasi-banking activities; they provide direct loans, credit guarantees, supply credit and prepayments for merchandise to their affiliated ventures.

Theoretically, the trading companies could, as commission merchants, intermediate trade transactions even without equity capital participation whenever and wherever such transactions take place in the open market (i.e., open-market intermediation). Alternatively, instead of waiting for some business opportunities to be created by manufacturers or others, the trading companies themselves could take the initiative of setting up their own manufacturing ventures so as to create and capture such transactional opportunities exclusively (i.e., closed-market intermediation). This is in fact the strategy the general trading companies have adopted overseas, particularly in developing countries, where they have been instrumental in transplanting labour-intensive ventures -- most frequently in co-operation with Japanese manufacturers and local interests.

They are thus much more the creators of new markets (transactional opportunities) than traditional middlemen, who are passive in this respect. In addition, the trading companies supply what may be called business infrastructure (23), such as warehousing, shipping, insurance, consulting, and financial services, to assist their transplanted manufacturing ventures in operating smoothly (evidence of this is given in Chapter VI). In this regard, they may also be called infrastructural entrepreneurs. Business infrastructures are just as much in short supply in the developing countries as physical infrastructures like irrigation, roads and communications facilities or social infrastructures, such as education and health.

40

When the nine traders are considered as a whole, textiles, metals and metal products, chemicals, and sundries are the four industries most frequently invested in. They account for 22.3 per cent, 19.6 per cent, 17.3 per cent, and 12.9 per cent, respectively. Taken together, they represent 72.1 per cent of the total number of manufacturing investments in which the trading companies are involved (see Annex 2, Table 5a).

Activities in textiles, both natural and synthetic, range from yarn-spinning and fabric-weaving to apparel making. Metals are mostly aluminium ingots, and metal products include such standardized products as rods, wires, plates, structural steel and galvanized iron sheets. The last item, in fact, is the single most important product; it alone accounts for 4.4 per cent of the total. Chemicals are similarly very standardized: printing ink, synthetic resins, agricultural chemicals (e.g., fertilizers, insecticide, herbicide, etc.), paint, dyes, adhesives, glues, caustic soda and plastic products. Sundries cover all those goods that are not classified under the other categories and include footwear (e.g., sport shoes and beach sandals), plywood, musical instruments, charcoal, cardboard boxes and paper products, toys, leather goods, bicycles and parts, furniture, and the like.

The investments in galvanized iron sheets deserve special attention. They were in fact among the very early manufacturing ventures the trading companies established in developing countries. There is a strong local demand for this technologically simple product, and the trading companies used to export it from Japan. But the developing countries soon imposed stiff tariffs and indicated their interest in producing it locally. The trading companies responded by setting up shop, usually in joint ventures with Japanese steel makers and local interests (Type D investments). These ventures proved to be quite profitable since the trading companies were still able to export iron sheets and to sell locally-galvanized ones at high prices under tariff protection (24).

The most common arrangement is one in which the traders hold at least an equal if not larger equity share than their Japanese manufacturing partner. Taken together, Japanese interests hold a minority ownership. But as technology is simple, trading companies sometimes set up shop even without the co-operation of a steel company. For example, Mitsui & Co. and C. Itoh jointly operate Sangkasi Thai Co. in Thailand with 500 workers. They hold 24 and 16 per cent interest respectively, and the balance (60 per cent) is held by local interests. All these ventures in galvanized iron sheets are of small-to-medium size in employment.

On the other hand, large-scale employment prevails in textile ventures involving such upstream operations as the production of staples and filaments, spinning and weaving, for they are usually dependent on a large-scale use of capital equipment in integrated production. For instance, some 3 300 workers are employed by First Synthetic Textiles, South Korea, a joint venture set up by Toray (24 per cent interest), Mitsui & Co. (6 per cent interest), and local interests (70 per cent). The venture produces polyester staples, yarns and polyester-rayon fabrics (25).

These large-scale textile investments are rather limited in number, however. In downstream textile operations, small-scale ventures are much more prevalent.

The pattern of sectoral concentration varies slightly from one company to the next. Marubeni, C. Itoh, Kanematsu Gosho, and Tomen are relatively more active in textiles than the others, whereas Sumitomo and Nissho-Iwai are relatively more active in metals and metal products, and Mitsui and Nichimen in Chemicals.

HIGH PROPENSITY TO TAKE ON LOCAL PARTNERS

It is clear that the trading companies have a high propensity to form joint ventures with local partners (Types C, C', D, and D'): together, these ventures account for a high 88.4 per cent, although the dominant form (66.3 per cent) is joint ventures involving a home office, a Japanese company and local or third-country interests (Type D). Since Type C ventures are those set up by traders and local interests without the participation of Japanese manufacturers, either the traders or the local partners must have the necessary manufacturing technologies. Type C ventures are therefore by and large limited to such unsophisticated, standardized technologies as food processing, textiles, (downstream operations) and metal products (see Annex 2 Table 5b).

Similarly, the lack of manufacturing skills on the part of trading companies is reflected in the rare occurrence of Types A and A' investments. They account for only 1.6 per cent and occur only in food processing, textiles and metal products, all technologically simple activities. Type B and B' investments cover all industrial sectors except iron and steel but occur only in host countries that are tolerant of wholly-owned foreign operations. Naturally, the same thing can be said of Type A and A' ventures.

The trading companies' high propensity to organise joint ventures with local partners is coupled with an equally high propensity to accept minority ownership (see Annex 2 Table 5c). The 10 to 29 per cent range of equity ownership is the most common, accounting for 47.9 per cent of the ventures, followed by the 1 to 9 per cent range (26.9 per cent of the ventures). Taken together, ventures with less-than-30 per cent equity ownership account for as much as 74.8 per cent. And this pattern applies equally to each of the nine trading companies.

Since trading companies work closely with their affiliated Japanese manufacturers as co-investors, one might suppose that Japanese interests, when combined, would represent majority ownership. However, even when we take into account Japanese interests as a whole, there is still a fairly high incidence of minority ownership, although it is less than that of the trading companies' shares alone (see Annex 2 Table 5d). Less than 50 per cent equity ownership accounts for slightly more than one half (52.3 per cent) of these manufacturing ventures, even though roughly one out of three are majority owned.

The trading companies' willingness -- and for that matter, the willingness of Japanese interests generally -- to remain as minority owners may be related in part to the comparatively small stakes involved in most of these manufacturing ventures. One would expect that the greater the absolute amount of capital invested, the more eager the investor to control management. The manufacturing ventures in which the trading companies participate as investors are in many cases of small-to-medium scale in operation. This is clearly demonstrated by the size of employment. The most frequently observed size in overseas ventures is the 100 to 299 employee range for the nine traders as a whole, accounting for 21.1 per cent. As pointed out earlier in this chapter, large-scale ventures with more than 1 000 employees do exist, but they represent only 8.9 per cent of the total number of the trading companies' manufacturing ventures abroad. In fact, large-scale ventures are less frequent than those with less than 50 workers, (14.2 per cent).

Moreover, trading companies are in a position to exercise a great deal of managerial control <u>without</u> holding majority ownership, since they provide such critical services <u>as supplies</u> of inputs and working capital and access to markets. It is thanks to these activities that they are able to earn commissions, overtly or covertly (that is, formally or in terms of transfer prices), a source of income as important, if not more so, than dividends from equity investments themselves. In fact, the former type of income can always be earned even if the overseas ventures operate in the red (that is, without any dividends).

CONCENTRATION IN THIRD WORLD COUNTRIES

Where are the trading companies' overseas manufacturing ventures located? More than half (53.4 per cent) are located in Asian countries (see Annex 2 Table 5e). Indonesia, Thailand, South Korea, Taiwan, Singapore, Malaysia, and the Philippines are among the most popular host countries. Latin American countries as a whole host about 20 per cent of the total. Brazil is the most popular host country for manufacturing ventures, not only in Latin America but also in the world: it alone accounts for 12 per cent. Africa and Middle East take about 8 per cent.

<u>Approximately 80 per cent of the trading companies' manufacturing ventures are concentrated in the developing countries.</u> This geographical concentration reflects the fact that most of these ventures produce standardized products in highly labour-intensive operations, both for local markets and for export, by capitalising on low-cost labour in Third World countries. It is also in the developing countries that the trading companies' ability to provide business-infrastructural services is in great demand and can create profitable opportunities for direct investment.

It should be remembered that when wages started to rise sharply in Japan and shortages of young factory workers became acute, particularly in the latter half of the 1960s, those manufacturers who had been operating in labour-intensive industrial sectors began to lose their trade competitiveness. It was the trading companies that took the initiative to encourage and assist them to relocate in relatively labour-abundant countries, and especially neighbouring Asian countries, by finding local partners and becoming joint investors themselves. All the characteristics we have described -- namely, a concentration of ventures in labour-intensive standardized products, a high propensity to form joint ventures with local interests, and geographical concentration in labour-abundant developing countries -- reflect the trading companies' great adaptability to a changing environment of production (factor-endowment conditions) at home.

There are some differences among companies, but they are slight: Sumitomo and Marubeni have a relatively large proportion of their manufacturing ventures in North America; C. Itoh, Marubeni, Nissho-Iwai, and Kanematsu tend to concentrate their manufacturing ventures in Latin America; while Tomen, Nichimen, Mitsui, and Mitsubishi have a relatively heavier concentration in Asia.

Two types of developing countries can be identified as host countries. The first are resource-scarce but labour-abundant countries, like South Korea, Taiwan, Singapore, and Hong Kong. The second are both resource- and labour-abundant countries like Brazil, Mexico, Indonesia, Malaysia and the Philippines. Interestingly enough, it is the small resource-scarce, labour-abundant Asian countries that initially attracted trading companies' manufacturing ventures, particularly during the 1960s and the early 1970s, and that succeeded in industrialising at impressively rapid rates. But as wages began to rise in these newly industrialising countries, trading companies shifted manufacturing activities to less developed, but both resource- and labour-abundant countries, especially Indonesia, Malaysia and the Philippines. This trend was also encouraged by a greater eagerness on the part of Japan to seek friendly relations with resource-rich countries in the aftermath of the first oil crisis in 1973. Some of these host countries have shown interest in attracting Japan's investments in small manufacturing as well as in resource-processing ventures and have specifically asked trading companies for such investments in addition to -- and often as a sort of implicit condition for -- their trading activities in resources. In this sense, some of the manufacturing ventures are set up as "semi-goodwill" ventures. In other words, if it were not for the attractiveness of crucial industrial resources which trading companies can profitably export home, they might not establish some manufacturing or processing ventures so readily.

A TENDENCY TO "PARCELLISE" VENTURES

One-half of all the ventures established up to 1980 were set up during the first half of the 1970s. Though the rate of increase decelerated in the second half of the 1970s, especially after the first oil crisis, some 77 per cent of the manufacturing ventures were set up during the decade (26).

This trend coincides with efforts made by trading companies to build transaction networks by establishing auxiliary trading ventures, an activity we examined in Chapter III. In fact, some auxiliary trading ventures were set up to support or in tandem with manufacturing ventures. Herein lies a curious feature of trading companies' overseas investment: manufacturing is often done independently from procurement or sales units, even though they deal with the same product and could easily be conceived as an integrated operation. For example, in Hong Kong, C. Itoh & Co. has four closely linked investments in joint ventures with Toray Industries, Japan's leading synthetic textile manufacturer, and local interests (27).

This fragmentation or "parcellisation" phenomenon of otherwise integral operations is also observed within manufacturing activities themselves. In the Philippines, for example, Nissho Iwai Corporation operates four vertically interrelated joint ventures in car production: two for the production of parts and components, one for assembly operation, and one for the import and sales of parts and components (28).

In fact, this tendency to parcellise a given manufacturing activity into separate but closely linked ventures is not necessarily limited to investments in which the trading companies participate. Some manufacturers adopt such a form of overseas investment, although it is perhaps more frequent with trading companies.

Why, then, do the trading companies (and Japanese manufacturers) often opt to parcellise -- rather than completely integrate (or internalise) -- their operations abroad? There are a number of possible reasons. First, they may simply be a reflection of their market structure at home. Major Japanese manufacturers usually have a cohort of subsidiaries or closely affiliated companies that serve as subcontractors or supply parts and components.

This vertical manufacturing system of closely co-ordinated operations by affiliated companies is called sangyo keiretsu. The best example of how it works is Japan's car industry. The major companies can economise on inventories and factory space because they can always count on "independent" subcontractors to bring in parts and components for assembly operations on time in a smoothly co-ordinated fashion. Since this system is considered to be one reason for Japan's industrial competitiveness, it is apt to be duplicated in its overseas investments.

Second, trading companies have a strong inclination to form joint ventures with local partners because, as we saw earlier, many of their manufacturing ventures are involved in technologically standardized products. They can therefore depend on local skills or alternatively bring in, either as co-investors or licensors, third parties that have the necessary technology. In choosing local partners, however, trading companies may encounter some difficulties, for in many cases there are several local interests (local elites) eager to enhance their positions by tying up with foreign multinationals, most notably in the developing countries. Hence trading companies are frequently compelled to simultaneously co-operate with several local elites for fear of antagonising them and more importantly for the sake of increasing their business and information linkages.

Trading companies are often helped by the fact that, as many of their manufacturing ventures are relatively simple in technology and small in scale, they can divide up either vertical or horizontal operations into a number of units so as to form joint ventures with various local interests. In this way, they can cover different stages of production or market territories, even though some may be more compactly integrated into one operation. This tendency is strong whenever a trading company is not quite sure which local interest will be the most suitable long-term partner.

The trading companies' strategy here is to minimise the possible risk associated with their manufacturing ventures and to maximise the span of their trading territories, that is, to set up as many affiliated manufacturing ventures as possible with minimum amounts of equity capital. This basic strategy results in their propensity to accept minority ownership but to build an extensive network of affiliated companies.

Equally as important in this connection is the fact that local elites, particularly in developing Asian countries, have traditionally been active in commercial capitalism for many centuries. They are careful not to put too many eggs in one basket, so to speak, and are prone to engage in short payoff ventures. Although they are now increasingly involved in industrial capitalism by becoming equity investors in manufacturing activities, their preference is still to diversify such investments as much as possible and not to tie up a large sum of capital in a few limited ventures. As a result, local partners themselves are often eager to form joint ventures.

Often, the reason may be much more straightforward: some local partners simply may not have enough capital to run an integrated, large-scale operation as majority owners. Hence they may end up taking a particular segment of production, say, to produce a certain type of part and component locally, with the rest of the necessary inputs imported from Japan. Later on, another segment of production may be localised with the establishment of another separate venture, either by the original investor or by other local interests. If this ad hoc incremental localisation continues, the result is a string of small parcellised operations.

This raises an interesting question with respect to the intrinsically different ways in which risks are minimised by commercial interests (whether trading companies or local commercial capitalists) on the one hand and by manufacturers on the other. Equity investments of commercial interests are diversified in a series of related ventures, whereas manufacturers are necessarily tied up in a particular line of activity. Although the trading companies' (or local commercial capitalists') tendency to parcellise local operations serves to maximise their own intermediating opportunities, does it not reduce the efficiency of manufacturing operations and raise risks in terms of possible disruptions in input supply and marketing activities? The answer seems to be yes, if local operations involve a series of integral production stages with possible scale economies but which happen to be parcellised. In most instances, however, the manufacturing ventures set up with trading companies as partners are relatively small-scale fabricating-processing, or assembly-type operations that do not entail much manufacturing risk or scale economies. Input supplies can be easily secured through alternative routes, and local operations are in fact more ideally managed in small separate units than on an integrated basis. Besides, productive inefficiency is usually tolerated to some extent because of high protective tariffs.

On the other hand, if local operations involve technologically sophisticated products requiring unified or integrated production, manufacturers usually do without trading companies as investment partners. In fact, as far as high-technology sectors are concerned, the "departure-from-traders" phenomenon has clearly taken place.

DIRECT OVERSEAS LOANS

Although trading companies usually take minority ownership in equity investment, they often extend a substantial amount of direct loans to their affiliated companies abroad, thereby becoming major creditors. This practice is certainly not new: as we saw in Chapter II, general trading companies are indeed regarded as financial intermediaries (quasi-bankers) by their affiliated companies at home. With the exception of Marubeni and Sumitomo, the major traders make more loans than equity investments. In 1979, for example, loans accounted for approximately 60 to 65 per cent of total equity and debt investments. The loan-equity ratio for Marubeni and Sumitomo was around 45 per cent and 35 per cent, respectively (see Annex 2 Table 2).

The trading companies' practice of giving loans at home has been extended to their overseas operations, though perhaps not to the same extent because of exchange risks and other constraints, especially in developing host countries. Yet the demand for such loans is particularly strong in capital-poor Third World countries. In many developing host countries, local partners apparently do not always have enough capital to pay up their portion of equity ownership, and loans from Japanese partners are actually used to finance equity investment (see Annex 2 Table 5f).

Most are long-term loans and are still outstanding. It is worth noting that a loan extended by a trading company to a particular venture is usually larger than the equity capital it invests. Herein lies the distinct strategy of trading companies to refrain from tying up a large amount of capital in the form of equity investment but instead to use direct loans flexibly and strategically to retain control of their affiliates. This type of arrangement no doubt constitutes "a new form of investment" on the international scene.

In fact, as will be seen in Chapter V, direct loans are made more frequently and in much larger amounts in connection with trading companies' efforts to secure overseas natural resources. According to one estimate, when all these loans are taken together, direct overseas loans most likely constitute about 20 per cent of the Top Nine traders' total overseas investments, including both equity and debt (29). Yet this estimate is only the tip of the iceberg: the overseas offices and subsidiaries of general trading companies are also quite active in raising funds to be lent to their overseas ventures. The Eurocurrency markets are no doubt an important source of finance. In fact, it is generally recognised that offshore-arranged loans are much larger and much more frequent than those secured directly from Japan, though unfortunately no comprehensive statistics are available. In addition, both the home offices of traders and their overseas offices very frequently provide loan guarantees for their affiliated ventures.

In short, the quasi-banking function of general trading companies serves as a strategic tool by which they exercise their control over flows of transactions emanating from a network of affiliated ventures. Their minority equity-ownership position for a particular overseas venture is often compensated for -- or even overcompensated for -- by their majority (or sole) creditor position.

There is another important reason for a relatively high incidence of joint ventures among Japanese manufacturing investments abroad. It has to do with the policy of the Japanese Government, as well as the consensual attitude of Japanese industry toward overseas investments in developing countries. The Japanese Government makes use of private investments as a form of economic assistance perhaps more consciously than the other industrial countries. In fact, private investments figure as a key component in official statistics of economic assistance to developing countries.

Although private overseas investments are carried out with a profit motive, they do transfer to the developing host country the vital ingredients of economic development -- capital, technology and access to markets. The Japanese Government believes that "market-co-ordinated" transfers are a more effective mechanism to encourage industrialisation than "politics-governed" transfers, so long as they are properly guided at the national level, that is, so long as the social benefits (and costs) to both the home and host countries are the criteria rather than profitable investments only.

Furthermore, overseas investments are clearly recognised as desirable from Japan's macro-economic point of view: a scarcity of resources, rising labour costs and industrial congestion at home, as well as trade frictions abroad, are all significant factors that compel Japan to move outward with investments. But most of these macroeconomic constraints (except trade frictions with the West) are often more readily removed by means of investments in developing countries than in advanced economies, a fact reflected by the heavy concentration of Japanese investments in the former rather than in the latter. And it is at this juncture that Japanese investments are frequently induced to take on the characteristics of economic aid, since developing host countries consider inflows of direct investment as an essential input for economic development, notably for their resource-based industrialisation.

It is on these grounds, indeed, that the Japanese Government is combining its official aid with the overseas advance of Japanese companies, especially in the area of resource development. It is urging the companies to accommodate themselves as much as possible to the needs of developing countries, including the use of joint ventures with local interests as a conduit of technology transfer. In other words, the social benefits of overseas investment are perceived to be much greater than its private benefits for both the home and host countries, a situation that justifies public financial assistance, both direct and indirect.

Japan's private sector has responded to this call for taking "social benefits" into consideration, partly because in so doing its private benefits are simultaneously enhanced with subsidies and other forms of assistance from both the Japanese and the host government. For example, the voluntary guidelines set forth in 1973 by the Japan Foreign Trade Council, an organisation composed of trading companies, specifies that their investments in developing countries ought to contribute to their host countries' economic development and national welfare and that, whenever possible, opportunities for local interests to participate in Japanese ventures should be created.

The most active among Japan's Government agencies in assisting publicly oriented (or "social-benefit-oriented") private ventures is the Overseas Economic Co-operation Fund (OECF), Japan's largest central aid-dispensing agency. This agency ties part of its aid money with private investments in large-scale ventures that the private sector alone cannot handle, for the most part in resource development and processing in collaboration with the host governments or their state enterprises. Some of these ventures are designated as "economic co-operation projects" by the Japanese Government (and frequently by the host governments simultaneously) because of their significance to the national welfare of both Japan and the host countries. The OECF usually becomes a major shareholder (with 30 to 40 per cent interest) of the Japanese investment consortium organised for such a venture, and the Japanese normally take 50 per cent or less ownership interest.

With substantial government assistance, the private costs of publicly-oriented investments are purposely kept below the social costs. From the point of view of national policy, this is justified because the social benefits of such investments in developing countries are considered much greater than the private benefits. This arrangement is perhaps responsible for making Japanese investors, particularly in large-scale overseas ventures, "more daring" and "more collaborative" with the host countries than they would otherwise be, and for that matter, even large Western corporations would be.

Unfortunately, however, this does not always produce a desirable result, for some huge long-term projects can be too eagerly pushed and too readily accepted without full consideration of all the future risks, partly because of government assistance and partly because of the nature of group investment.

The Mitsui group's petrochemical complex at Bandar Khomeni in Iran, for example, was pushed forward at the initiative of Mitsui & Co. It was to have a production capacity of 3.2 million tons of petrochemical products, the largest such facility in the Middle East. It was designed to influence the Iranian Government in order to secure favourable supplies of oil, which was considered a social benefit for all of Japan's industries. About 80 per cent of the construction had been completed but, at the height of the political turmoil, work came to a halt. Iraqi bombings damaged the site. Nonetheless, in August 1979, the Japanese Government, in view of the importance of Iranian oil (which accounted for some 17 per cent of Japan's oil imports prior to the revolution), designated the complex as an economic co-operation project, promising financial support from the OECF. Thereupon the Mitsui group began to organise an expanded Japanese investment consortium by inviting 78 companies to co-invest. Despite all these efforts, the project is in abeyance and the prospects look grim. Even though the Mitsui group and the Iranians have already sunk $2 billion into the project, it will probably be written off.

This unfortunate development has dampened the enthusiasm not only of the Mitsui group but also of other industrial groups for large-scale investment projects in Third World countries, although they are still called upon to participate because of their capacity to serve as project organisers (or as infrastructural entrepreneurs). In fact, even the OECF is now more cautious about promoting such huge ventures. Instead it is encouraging medium-scale projects, which it backs up either with direct loans to the developing countries or loans to the private Japanese companies, rather than through equity participation in Japanese investment consortiums.

The OECF is, however, committed to two other huge petrochemical projects now under construction. One is a $1.5 billion petrochemical complex to be completed at Al Jubail in Saudi Arabia by the Mitsubishi group (with the Mitsubishi Corporation as leader). It is a 50-50 joint venture with Saudi Arabian Basic Industries. The Japanese investment consortium, called Saudi Petro-Chemicals Development Co., is composed of 54 Japanese companies and the OECF, the latter being its major shareholder. The other project is a $800 million petrochemical complex now under construction on a small island off Singapore; it is organised by the Sumitomo group in a joint venture with the Singapore Government. Its Japanese consortium consists of 23 companies and the OECF as the major shareholder. The future of these two projects is uncertain, however, because of the depressed market prospects for their products. (Government support will be discussed further in Chapter V).

ASSESSMENT

The overseas manufacturing ventures set up by the general trading companies, whether alone or jointly with others, are concentrated in technologically standardized, relatively labour-intensive industries, such as textiles, metal products, basic chemicals and sundries. Most of these ventures are small in scale and are located in developing countries, especially in Asia. Their operations are on the whole congruent with local conditions, in the sense that their labour-intensive production matches the host countries' overall factor endowments characterised by labour abundance.

The production technologies and skills transplanted through these ventures from Japan to the developing host countries are for the most part standardized. By advanced countries' standards, they may seem "obsolete", but they are still commercially viable and quite effective in developing countries. In this respect, trading companies can be looked upon as intermediaries for transplanting "locally congruent" industrial technologies in developing host countries -- not in "disembodied" form (that is, through licensing agreements) but in "embodied" form (that is, through joint ventures and through the installation of machinery and equipment).

There is no doubt that the trading companies have played a key role in promoting Japan's overseas investments in labour-intensive industries. For example, as much as 65 per cent of Japan's overseas ventures in the textile industry (from fibre and fabric to apparel and fishing nets) have been set up either by trading companies (not only the Top Nine traders but also smaller traders) either by themselves or jointly with other interests (30). Given their dominant position, it would not be amiss to argue that Japan's generally high propensity to engage in new forms of investment, especially minority ownership in joint ventures and the frequent use of direct overseas loans is a reflection of the trading companies' operative characteristics.

The trading companies' investments in manufacturing were most actively carried out in the early 1970s, up till the first oil crisis, when the Japanese economy was at the height of its phenomenal expansion. The oil crisis and the subsequent slowdown of the economy constrained the trading companies' investment activities. Furthermore, Japanese industry began in earnest to introduce industrial robots in labour-intensive operations so as to cut down on costs at home. To some extent these labour-saving innovations must have served as substitutes for overseas manufacturing investments designed to capitalise on low-cost labour in developing countries.

Japan's industrial structure also began to shift away from raw material- or energy-intensive sectors toward more knowledge-intensive ones. It was against the backdrop of these abrupt changes in Japan's industrial environment that the general trading companies found their business opportunities shrinking, for their traditional intermediating activities were closely tied to declining industrial sectors.

At the same time, some developing countries, especially rapidly industrialising ones, started to emphasize the development of technology-intensive industries, such as electronics, with the help of foreign capital and technology. They were no longer as interested in or capable of hosting labour-intensive ventures because of rising wages. In other words, these host countries became less enthusiastic about the type of manufacturing investments trading companies had so far been able to promote.

All these developments both at home and overseas were no doubt responsible for the recent decline in the rate of increase in labour-intensive manufacturing ventures set up by trading companies. Consequently, the general trading companies are at the moment endeavouring to diversify their trading activities at home into high-technology growth sectors -- computers, office automation equipment, robots, and biotechnology -- to compensate for a severe stagnation in basic-materials industries (steel, aluminium, oil, sugar and the like) in which they have been traditionally most active as traders.

Mitsubishi Corporation, for example, recently concluded a basic agreement for a business tie-up with IBM of Japan to develop a new information industry. Sumitomo Corporation has established a foot-hold in factory automation by making a joint business arrangement with Nippon Electric Co. and a leading industrial robot firm. Meanwhile, C. Itoh, Kanematsu Gosho and Nissho-Iwai have been active in reallocating their manpower resources toward such high-technology sectors as space, aircraft, electronics and telecommunications.

It remains to be seen, however, whether the trading companies will actually succeed in capturing these new growth sectors and how their success, if attained, will affect their overseas investment activities. As high-technology sectors flourish in high-income markets, trading companies' overseas investments will most likely be oriented towards advanced or rapidly industrialising economies rather than developing countries in these fields.

Chapter V

OVERSEAS RESOURCE DEVELOPMENT VENTURES

The Japanese economy experienced a rapid structural shift away from light manufacturing industries towards heavy and chemical industries during the postwar period, and up to the oil crisis. Demands for industrial resources soared, sometimes at a rate of nearly 20 per cent per year and in any case much faster than the overall economic growth rate, which itself was impressively high, at more than 10 per cent per year. As Japan severely lacked natural resources, economic development led to a gigantic increase in imports of overseas resources. The country soon became the world's leading importer of iron ore, copper, aluminium, coal, timber and grains (see Annex 2 Table 6a). Since it was the trading companies that imported resources, rising imports naturally expanded their business opportunities.

We shall begin by examining how Japan secured vital supplies of overseas resources in the postwar period and show how its strategy changed by looking successively at five periods: the 1950s; the first half of the 1960s; the second half of the 1960s; the early 1970s (prior to the oil crisis); and the post-oil-crisis period (from the mid-1970s to the present).

During the 1950s, Japan was totally dependent on the open market, and mainly spot markets, for overseas resources. Japan's position as a resource importer was not yet significant, for it was still in the early stages of building its heavy and chemical industries. At this point, more domestically available resources -- coal and hydro-electric power -- were being consumed than imported ones, although the use of oil both as an industrial raw material and fuel gradually began to rise. It was not till the second half of the 1950s, for example, that Japan's petrochemical industry came into existence and that imported oil began to become significant as a raw material.

The first half of the 1960s saw the beginning of Japan's effort to secure supplies by means of direct investments in overseas resources, but they were significant neither in number nor in scale. These ventures were carried out by trading companies, steel producers and smelters rather sporadically and in an ad hoc manner. Japan continued to rely on spot-market purchases, since supplies were relatively abundant and secure; resource markets were still firmly controlled by major Western companies and prices remained attractively low for industrial users. In fact, the overall price trend was downward. Given the stability of resource markets, Japanese industry concentrated on reducing transport costs by building mammoth tankers and ore carriers, which were able to exploit scale economies in transportation and further reduce the cost of imported resources.

The second half of the 1960s. By the mid-1960s, Japan was well on the way to transforming its industrial structure, which was to become dominated by the heavy and chemical manufacturing sectors. This structural transformation continued to gather momentum during the rest of the decade. Japan overtook one European economy after another in gross national product and emerged as the Number Two industrial power after the United States in the Free World. It was also during this period that Japan became the world's largest importer of resources. Ironically, one of the world's least resource-endowed countries, came to have the highest concentration of industrial activity in sectors consuming the most resources and the lowest concentration in those requiring the least resources.

As a result of this enormous rise in Japan's dependence on overseas resources -- and a much greater vulnerability to disruptions in resources markets -- Japanese industry began to step up its effort to secure supply sources through overseas investments. Japanese investors pushed not only for the "loan-and-import" type of resource development (in which loans are extended to resource suppliers at concessionary interest rates in exchange for supply contracts for resources) but also for the "invest-and-import" type, in which equity participation is made to secure supplies. Among them were the general trading companies, who usually formed investment groups.

The first half of the 1970s saw the most rapid growth in Japan's overseas resource-development ventures, partly because of the very favourable balance-of-payments conditions, which led to a sharp appreciation of the Japanese currency. This created an indirect subsidy effect on overseas investment. The Japanese Government also adopted a "yen defence" programme which included encouraging overseas capital outflows in order to prevent a further appreciation of the currency. Japan's economy continued to grow briskly until the first oil crisis of 1973, and its search -- and reach -- for overseas resources intensified.

As the increasing scale of operation for overseas resource development entailed greater capital requirements (hence greater financial risks), the Japanese Government became more involved in assisting the private sector in such ventures. It was during this period that the concept of "national projects" was formalized. The so-called Asahan project, an aluminium smeltery in Indonesia, which we shall describe later on, was the first to be launched, with heavy financial assistance from both the Japanese and Indonesian Governments.

The second half of the 1970s. (After the first oil crisis in 1973), the Japanese economy slowed down considerably, as did its overseas investment activities. But the oil crisis served to drive home the vulnerability of Japan's reliance on overseas resources and the strategic importance of diversifying its supply sources. In its search for energy resources, Japan began turning to non-Arab sources like Indonesia and Mexico, and to politically stable and open economies like Australia, the United States and Canada.

So-called "resource diplomacy" came into play as the Japanese Government became more involved through such agencies as the Overseas Economic Co-operation Fund (OECF), the Japan International Co-operation Agency (JICA), the Export-Import Bank of Japan (EX-Im Bank), the Japan Petroleum Development Corporation (JPDC), the Overseas Mineral Resources Development Corporation (OMRDC), and the Overseas Fishery Co-operative Foundation (OFCF) (31).

Towards the end of the decade the Japanese yen once again appreciated sharply, creating what was called in Japan "a second boom" of overseas invest-ment (the "first boom" having occurred in the early 1970s). In 1979, invest-ments in resource development jumped to $1 011 million, a $550 million or 119.3 per cent increase over the previous year. Of that increase $31 million went to agriculture, forestry, and fishery, and $519 million to the mining and fuel extraction sector (32).

FROM IMPORT AGENT TO DEVELOPMENT AGENT

As we saw in Chapter II, trading companies were originally fostered by the Japanese Government after the Meiji Restoration not only to export Japanese goods to earn foreign exchange but also to import resources from overseas at the lowest possible cost by avoiding the intermediation of foreign traders. Japan's trading companies were thus a crucial instrument for a national policy of import substitution in overseas trading services.

As a result, and by what came to be a unique feature of Japan's indus-trial groups, the major users of industrial resources, like steel makers and smelters, came to depend on trading companies for their supply of industrial resources. "Shoken" (the commercial right to intermediate) was created, whereby each user purchased a given resource through the intermediation of a particular trading company and paid it a commission. For the import of iron ore and coking coal, for example, the trading companies literally enjoy a monopoly (see Annex 2 Table 6b) and we may state that in Japan there is no open market to speak of for these imported resources.

The major suppliers of iron ore for Japan Steel are, in order of ranking, Mitsui, Nissho Iwai, Mitsubishi, Marubeni and C. Itoh; for Nippon Kokan, the suppliers are Marubeni and Mitsubishi; for Kawasaki Steel are C. Itoh, Mitsubishi, and Mitsui; for Sumitomo Metal are Sumitomo and Mitsubishi; for Kobe Steel are Nissho Iwai, Marubeni, Mitsubishi and Mitsui; and for Nisshin Steel Mitsubishi, Mitsui, and Nissho Iwai. On the other hand, for Tomen, Nippon Kokan is the most important customer; and for both Kanematsu and Nichimen, Japan Steel is their foremost customer.

Not surprisingly, a very similar pattern emerges for the supply of coking coal (see Annex 2 Table 6c). Tables 6b and 6c provide clear evidence of the close-knit relationships established thanks to shoken between the trading companies and the major resource users.

COMMODITY PATTERN

The trading companies' investments in resource extraction are heavily concentrated in the development of iron ore (15.1 per cent of the total number of their resource development ventures; (see Annex 2 Table 7a), followed by coal (9.4 per cent). These findings are not surprising in view of the trading companies' monopolistic position as suppliers of these resources to Japanese industry. Non-ferrous metals, which include copper, zinc, lead, bauxite, nickel and tin, account for 23 per cent. But, on an item-by-item basis, each of these non-ferrous metals is less significant than either iron ore or coal as far as trading companies' overseas investment is concerned, since the companies do not control the domestic markets for non-ferrous metals. The protection of shoken and the accompanying obligation for traders to provide stable supplies goes a long way to explain their efforts to set up direct investments in overseas resource development.

By comparison, the trading companies' ventures in oil and natural gas are relatively small in number (accounting for only 4.3 per cent) and have till now been less actively pursued (although some companies are beginning to show more interest). Apparently, a major constraint on Japan's direct investments in this field is the relatively small number of development engineers.

On the company level, Sumitomo Corporation is particularly active in non-ferrous metals, which reflects the nature of the Sumitomo group to which the trading company belongs. As explained in Chapter II, the Sumitomo zaibatsu was originally built around Japan's once-famed (but now closed) copper mine in Besshi.

The trading companies are also setting up ventures in agribusiness (mainly plantation, animal husbandry and the dairy business), fishery (often including processing, freezing and canning), and forestry and lumber. Mitsui, Mitsubishi, C. Itoh, and Marubeni are by far the most active group of developers. This again reflects their market positions at home: in foodstuffs, for example, the market shares of Mitsui and Mitsubishi stand at 20 per cent each. C. Itoh accounts for 15 per cent, and Marubeni 13 per cent, while the shares of Sumitomo, Nissho Iwai, Tomen, Kanematsu, and Nichimen range from 4 to 9 per cent each (33).

TYPES OF VENTURES IN RESOURCE DEVELOPMENT

The trading companies most frequently opt for joint ventures (34), which account for 48.2 per cent. These tripartite ventures in minerals and fuels often include third-country parties, namely big Western multinationals, as joint investors, although third-country parties are not found in agriculture, fishery, or forestry.

The next most popular type is bilateral joint ventures between a trading company and local interests (types C and C'), which account for 30.9 per cent. These bilateral ventures usually involve equity capital participation in existing foreign companies rather than setting up entirely new companies. The ventures that include local partners (types C, C', D and D') account for almost 80 per cent.

There are 16 wholly-owned ventures (11.5 per cent), most of them prospecting or exploration projects in minerals and fuels. This particular stage of activity does not require much capital investment and can be carried out on a small scale, hence trading companies can often take on the job themselves by hiring independent prospectors and other specialists.

It is worth noting that, compared with other sectors, most of the regional offices of the trading companies have not been active investors in resource development. For one, they are strongly oriented towards their home market (developed resources are shipped to Japanese markets). A second reason is that, because of the huge capital requirements, for which the government often provides assistance, these ventures are controlled by the home offices of the trading companies (35).

Some specific examples of these major types of investment are as follows:

-- Iron Ore Company of Alaska, U.S.A., is a Type A wholly-owned subsidiary of Mitsubishi Corporation engaged in surveying and exploring iron ore mines. It is capitalised at $2.3 million.

-- Eastern Atlantic Iron Ore Co., Bahamas, is a Type B joint venture owned by Mitsubishi Corporation (50.6 per cent), Nippon Kokan (15.4 per cent), Kobe Steel (15.4 per cent), Nisshin Steel (10.8 per cent), and Kawasaki Steel (7.8 per cent). The company mines iron ore and produces pellets. It is capitalised at 76.3 million Bahamian dollars.

-- Consolidated Mines, the Philippines, is a Type C venture between a local mining company and Marubeni (2.8 per cent). It is engaged in the extraction and marketing of non-ferrous metals.

-- Empreendimentos Brasileiros de Mineracao S.A., Brazil, is a Type D investment company set up by Japanese interests (20 per cent) in collaboration with local interests (80 per cent). It invests specifically in iron ore mines. The Japanese group consists of Sumitomo Corporation, C. Itoh & Co., Japan Steel, Nippon Kokan, Sumitomo Metal, Kawasaki Steel, Kobe Steel, Nisshin Steel, and others.

The last example is typical of group investments in which more than one trading company enters into a joint investment on the Japanese side. Group investment of this type is frequent in overseas resource development, for the minimum investment is usually large. As pointed out in Chapter I, the aggregate statistics for investments made by the nine trading companies given in this study should therefore be understood as the total number of investment participations rather than the total number of companies established overseas.

It should also be stressed that although their equity shares in group investments may be relatively small, trading companies often play a crucial role as project organisers. True, the initiative for resource development projects may not always come from trading companies. It is the big users of resources, like steel makers and metal smelters, that frequently initiate such projects. But sooner or later trading companies are likely to be brought in as co-investors since they do provide critical services -- project coordination, procurement of plants, and distribution of output.

INVESTMENT TREND

The trading companies, and especially the top five, began to invest in overseas resource development in the 1960s. By the first half of the 1970s, all the nine trading companies were busily setting up resource development ventures. During this five-year period, half of all the ventures that came to be established prior to 1980 were set up. The trading companies continued to advance in the second half of the 1970s, but only at a much slower pace; nonetheless the majority (74.1 per cent) of all ventures were established in the 1970s.

LOCATION

As could be expected, Oceania, and particularly Australia, is the region with the most ventures (24.9 per cent), notably in minerals and coal. Asia ranks second with 23 per cent, and Latin America (particularly Brazil) ranks third, with 18 per cent, followed by Canada and the United States. Overall, one half of these ventures are located in developing regions.

OWNERSHIP

The trading companies' high propensity to be minority shareholders is slightly less strong in resource development than in manufacturing. The 10 to 29 per cent range is the most frequent (31.7 per cent), and less than 50 per cent ownership accounts for as much as 76.3 per cent. Ownership of even less than 1 per cent occurs in one out of every ten cases (10.1 per cent), which is a striking illustration of the trading companies' strategy in resource development. This preference for minority ownership indicates, as we pointed out earlier, their strategy to minimise financial involvement (risk) in each venture but to maximise the opportunities to create new shoken and scale economies in intermediation by affiliating themselves with as many ventures as possible.

As trading companies often tie up with the Japanese users of imported resources, like steel makers, in overseas resource development, what is the real ownership of Japanese interests? Majority ownership of 80 to 100 per cent is quite frequent (30.9 per cent), but minority ownership of less than 29 per cent interest is more frequent, accounting for 34.5 per cent. Slightly more than one out of every two cases are less than 50 per cent ownership (53.9 per cent frequency). Thus a relatively high propensity to accept minority interest on the part of Japanese group investors is clearly discernible.

ILLUSTRATIONS OF RESOURCE DEVELOPMENT VENTURES

A few ventures are worth being singled out and described in detail for they illustrate the salient features of resource development ventures initiated or participated in by trading companies:

In 1963 Mitsubishi Corporation conceived the plan for a liquified natural gas project and, in partnership with Royal Dutch Shell Oil and the Government of Brunei (formerly Northwest Borneo), it set up Brunei LNG (liquefied natural gas) Ltd. in 1969. As a minority shareholder with 33.3 per cent, Mitsubishi invested $90 million, which was a large amount of capital for a trading company to commit at the time. In 1972 the first shipments were made to Japan, where Mitsubishi sells to the electric power and gas companies under a long-term contract. It has a 20-year contract to buy 5 million tons of LNG annually from the Brunei company.

Because of the sharp rise in the price of liquefied natural gas, Mitsubishi's investment has proved to be enormously profitable. It now yields an annual dividend of some 20 billion yen, or roughly $80 million (36) and is considered to be Mitsubishi's biggest "dollar box". (As a result, Mitsubishi continues to enjoy a high rate of return on its overall equity investment, with an average rate of 9.4 per cent as compared with an average of 2.8 per cent for the nine trading companies, as we saw in Chapter II). Thanks to this foresighted investment, Mitsubishi now dominates the import market for liquefied natural gas and has invested in such other development projects as the Sarawak LNG venture in Malaysia (in which it holds 17.5 per cent interest, Shell 17.5 per cent, and PETRONAS 65 per cent). Mitsubishi Corporation's success naturally stimulated the interest of other trading companies in resource extraction.

The Robe River Iron Ore Co. of Australia is another successful venture, thanks to the organisational skills of Mitsui & Co. with Cliff's Western Australian Mining Co., Robe River Ltd. and Mt. Enid Iron Co. as co-investors, Mitsui holds a 30 per cent interest. The Mitsui interest is in turn controlled by the Mitsui Iron Ore Development Co. of Australia, a subsidiary set up by Mitsui home office (80 per cent interest) and its Australian office (20 per cent interest).

This venture is engaged in mining iron ore that was once considered too poor in quality to be of any commercial use. But Mitsui & Co. realised that a special technology owned by the Cleveland Cliff Iron Co. (USA) would make the iron ore usable, and succeeded in acquiring it for the venture.

The project, initiated in 1969, included the construction of 168 kilometres of railroad track, port facilities to accommodate 150 000-ton class ore carriers and a new company mining town for workers. So far $400 million have been invested, with Mitsui contributing for 78.36 million ($8.16 million in equity capital and $70.2 million in loans).

Shipments to Japan began in 1972. The mine produces 14 million tons of pulverized iron ore (of which 8 million tons are exported to Japan) and 5 million tons of pellets (of which 4.2 million tons are exported to Japan). Mitsui has 15-year supply contracts with Japan's six major steel makers (Japan Steel, Nippon Kokan, Kawasaki Steel, Sumitomo Metal, Kobe Steel, and Nisshin Steel). This project has without doubt helped make Mitsui the foremost supplier of iron ore in Japan. Moreover, the Robe River project was the first venture in which a trading company succeeded in developing a profitable iron ore mine by taking on both exploration and marketing risks without the participation of Japanese users.

In 1969 Mitsui & Co. opened P.T. Mitsugoro, an agricultural plantation in South Sumatra, Indonesia, to raise corn in a joint venture with Kosgoro, a local agricultural co-operative. It wanted to introduce a high-grade corn, teach farming skills, and establish an integrated production and marketing system. Initially, Mitsui held 51 per cent interest, and Kosgoro 49 per cent interest, but later on Mitsui became the majority owner (95.4 per cent).

Although this venture has not been commercially successful, it is considered to be a valuable regional development project that contributes to the welfare of the local community. (The company's highest in-house award -- the "Mitsui President Award" -- was given to the project director). And Mitsui has been subsidising the project in the spirit of economic co-operation with Indonesia, although it is now negotiating the transfer of the project to the Indonesian Government.

Davao Fruits Corporation, in the Philippines, is a banana plantation jointly established by Sumitomo Corporation (36 per cent interest) and local interests (64 per cent). Launched in 1971, the plantation covers 3 000 hectares and employs nearly 3 500 local workers. Only two Japanese (one executive and one technical advisor) are stationed there. All the bananas produced are exported to Japan under the brand name of "Bananbo". It is regarded as a successsful -- and for Sumitomo, a commercially viable -- regional development venture. Japan completely liberalised banana imports in 1963, and demand has been growing steadily.

It is worth noting that all Japan's banana imports from the Philippines are intermediated by Japan's trading companies, including some small ones: C. Itoh is an import agent for Standard Fruits; Fuji Fruits, Toyata Tshusho, and Tokyo Seika for Del Monte; Kyokuto Fruits for United Brands; and Tomen and Zen Nikko Shoji for small banana growers (37).

The Asahan aluminium project -- construction of a hydro-electric power station on the Asahan river in Indonesia, an aluminium refinery that uses the power generated, and related infrastructural facilities -- draws together seven trading companies as co-investors (Mitsui & Co., Mitsubishi Corporation, Sumitomo Corporation, C. Itoh & Co., Marubeni Corporation, Nissho Iwai, and Nichimen Jitsugyo), although the project itself was originally conceived and brought to the implementation stage by five major smelters (Showa Denko, Japan Light Metal, Sumitomo Chemical, Mitsubishi Chemical, and Mitsui Aluminium). Initially, several Western multinational corporations participated in an international bidding, but they withdrew when they learned that the host government wanted to make the project a comprehensive regional development scheme that would include infrastructural facilities (port and highways). In spite of the huge financial requirement of the project, Japanese industry thus became the only partner for the Indonesian Government.

Immediately after the first oil crisis, the Japanese Government officially supported the project in the hope of securing Indonesian oil, and the venture was designated as "an economic co-operation project" that was entitled to receive official financial aid. The Suharto Government of Indonesia staked its credibility on the project by turning it into a pivotal regional economic development programme. Political and economic interests on both sides finally coalesced, and a formal contract was signed in 1975.

At present the refinery is 90 per cent owned by Japanese interests, but in ten years 25 per cent of the total shares will be transferred to the Indonesian Government. The hydroelectric power station, with a capacity of 430 000 kilowatts, will be turned over to the Indonesian Government after 30 years of operation. Training programmes for local operatives are part and parcel of the project. Hence the project could be considered as a kind of long-term turnkey operation.

Official Japanese finance covers 70 per cent of the total cost of the project: loans for the aluminium refinery came from the Export-Import Bank; for the power station from the OECF; and for a port, highways, and other overhead facilities from JICA. Loans from Japanese commercial banks cover an additional 20 per cent. The balance of 10 per cent, the initial Indonesian share, is paid by the host government.

Although the Asahan venture is a project organised by resource-users, the participating trading companies are expected to play a crucial role in marketing aluminium once production gets underway. The project also set an important precedent for Japan's resource diplomacy: the Asahan formula -- capital participation of the Japanese Government by way of its official agencies, along with that of resource users and trading companies in a large-scale overseas project -- was applied to other resource-related ventures, such as the huge petrochemical projects in Iran, Saudi Arabia and Singapore, as we saw in Chapter IV.

INDIRECT EQUITY INVESTMENT

Trading companies' equity investments in overseas resource development are actually much larger than what has been described so far. They are also joint shareholders -- and sometimes even majority shareholders -- in various resource development corporations headquartered in Japan. For example, there are six uranium exploration and development corporations and seven petroleum development corporations in which the trading companies participate (see Annex 2 Tables 7b and 7c).

The uranium exploration companies were organised at the initiative of the trading companies, which are usually the major shareholders. Although they take the form of joint ventures, the number of partners is rather limited. On the other hand, the petroleum development companies were established by major industrial groups with a large number of co-investors, and the trading companies generally invest as a member of their respective group.

DIRECT OVERSEAS LOAN

So far we have examined only equity capital investments or the "invest-and-import" type of resource development ventures. But trading companies also extend direct loans to overseas resource developers in connection with either their long-term purchase contracts or their collaborative efforts to search for and develop new sources of resource supplies, such as mines and wells. This activity was referred to earlier as the "loan-and-import" type of resource development. Loans may be combined with equity capital investments or may simply be extended to non-affiliated foreign resource producers.

Mitsubishi Corporation is the most active in extending such loans, accounting for about 35 per cent, which are fairly concentrated in North America and Asia. Mitsui & Co. ranks second, with a large proportion of its loans extended to Asia and Oceania. Then come C. Itoh & Co., Sumitomo Corporation and Nissho Iwai with an equal number of loans. Taken together, these five traders account for 87 per cent of all direct overseas loans. Overall, Asia (especially Indonesia) is the most frequent recipient of resource-development loans (35 per cent). North America and Latin America rank second, each accounting for 22 per cent. They are followed by Oceania, and especially Australia (see Annex 2 Table 7d).

More than half these loans are of the "pure" loan-and-import type, that is, they are extended to independent resource producers overseas, and the trading companies have no equity interest. The rest of the loans are combined with the invest-and-import type (i.e., they are given to those overseas ventures in which the trading companies have equity participation). Yet there are some differences among the nine traders. Middle-ranking Marubeni, C. Itoh, Sumitomo, and Nissho Iwai are more active in lending to independent foreign resource producers than to their affiliated ones, while the two largest, Mitsui and Mitsubishi, are either just as active or more so in lending to their affiliated ventures. On the other hand, the smallest ones, Tomen and Nichimen, lend only to their affiliated ventures.

Copper ore ranks first (37 per cent) in direct resource development loans, far exceeding iron ore, which comes second (17 per cent). Thus these two resources alone account for 54 per cent of resource-development loans. There is a close relation between this pattern and the fact that, in 1979, Japan secured approximately 50 per cent of the copper ore and 30 per cent of the iron ore it imported under loan-and-import arrangements (38). This is no coincidence, because trading companies are the major resource procurers for Japanese industry. Agribusiness, fishing and forestry account for 28 per cent, a fairly large proportion of the traders' direct loans extended from Japan (see Annex 2 Table 7e).

Big loans exceeding 10 billion yen are made by the two largest traders, Mitsui and Mitsubishi, but most frequently loans run to less than 1 billion yen (46 per cent) and between 1 billion and 5 billion yen (26 per cent) (39).

As the primary aim is to secure stable, long-term supplies of resources for Japan, these loans are usually offered on a concessional basis, with interest rates pegged lower than the going market rate and with favourable repayment schedules, including grace periods. The trading companies usually borrow funds from Japan's city banks as well as from the Export-and-Import Bank of Japan, which matches the commercial loans on favourable terms. In some cases loans are so arranged that repayments are made not in money but in the natural resources that trading companies agree to acquire.

In addition to loans extended directly from Japan, trading companies also make offshore-arranged loans to foreign resource suppliers. The sources of offshore-arranged loans include the flotation of debentures overseas by trading companies' regional headquarters (say, Mitsui & Co., U.S.A), borrowings from foreign banks, and retained earnings of their locally incorporated overseas ventures. The general trading companies' capacity to raise funds abroad has expanded considerably in recent years because their credit standings, including those of their regional offices, are now rated quite high in overseas financial markets.

Unfortunately, statistics on offshore-arranged loans are not available, but the top-ranking traders are certainly more capable of -- hence more active in -- raising funds abroad than the low-ranking ones. Offshore-arranged loans have been on the rise in recent years (although there are wide fluctuations in such arrangements depending upon interest-rate differentials between Tokyo and foreign financial centres). The trading companies also provide credit guarantees when their overseas ventures borrow from financial intermediaries.

Japanese traders often show preference for the loan-and-import approach rather than the pure invest-and-import approach, for they are growing increasingly wary of committing large sums of capital to foreign extractive projects. In general, resource producers suffer not only a long-term deterioration in their terms of trade but also wide short-term price fluctuations. As a result they often operate in the red in a depressed market. Yet even when debtors' operations are in the red, interest is always paid even though interest incomes are certainly not the primary purpose of such loans. Furthermore, direct loans are not likely to be "expropriated", whereas equity investments are subject to such risk. And resource-purchase-linked loans are not likely to be defaulted either, for the debtor can always pay off, if not in money then in resources, which after all are the ultimate object of such loans. This also means that the debtor does not need to worry about debt rescheduling and a deterioration of his credit rating. For host countries, direct loans are a form of unpackaged investment since they are obtaining only needed working capital and access to markets -- vital services that are "unbundled" from other services which they themselves can provide. Thus overseas direct loans are a "new" form of investment, perhaps increasingly welcomed by both resource buyers and suppliers.

ASSESSMENT

Japan's major trading companies enjoy monopsonistic positions in securing vital industrial resources and foodstuffs from overseas, partly as a result of the commercial tradition dating back to the Meiji period. The trading companies also operate very closely -- if not exclusively -- with the member companies of their respective industrial groups. These unique features of Japanese industry enable them to create "shoken", or the commercial right to intermediate in trade. Indeed, trading companies monopolise the import and distribution channels for iron ore, coking coal, and other mineral resources, as well as grains -- albeit in a climate of fierce rivalry.

Given their role as exclusive importers of key resources, it is natural that once Japan's demands had grown so great that open market purchases were no longer appropriate to secure supplies at stable prices, trading companies began to invest in resource development ventures abroad in collaboration with major resource users. Throughout the 1950s and the 1960s Japan depended on Western resource suppliers -- the "majors" -- who firmly controlled their production bases throughout the world and were able to deliver resources at relatively low prices. In the early 1970s, however, the emergence of economic nationalism, particularly in Third World countries, and which was dramatised by OPEC's action, drastically altered the global equation of resource supplies. The Western majors began to lose their grip on supply sources. Japan therefore began to pursue in earnest so-called "resource diplomacy", focussing its diplomatic effort on resource-abundant countries, particularly in the Third World.

Since resource development ventures require a relatively long period of exploration and large-scale extractive operations, organisational skills to conduct feasibility studies, to set up extractive facilities, to co-ordinate production and to market extractive resources are obviously required. It is in this context that the general trading companies' global networks of information and marketing and their capacity to raise capital and to serve as project organiser/co-ordinators came to be recognised and their services called for. In turn, the trading companies themselves are eagerly taking advantage of this new economic opportunity, so much so that there is even talk of the possible emergence of the general trading companies as "Japanese majors" in the world resource market.

The first half of the 1970s saw the most vigorous surge of investment activities in resource development by trading companies, but the global recession following the oil crisis of 1973 slowed down their advance. The Iranian Revolution brought a halt to Mitsui's huge petrochemical complex project, which was an enormous financial loss to the company. As a result, and despite their eagerness to take up their new role as organisers of large-scale overseas projects, the trading companies have grown more cautious about Third-World projects and are seeking much greater co-operation and financial support from the Japanese Government. To avoid risks they are also re-directing more of their investment activities towards politically stable, resource-rich advanced countries like Canada, the United States and Australia.

Trading companies are in essence project organisers or participants, whose main interest is to establish a long-lasting affiliation with a given resource project with a minimal amount of equity capital participation. This is a very different approach from that of traditional investors, whose major goal is to control ownership and management through 100 per cent or majority ownership and by completely internalising market transactions within their organisations. The traders' aim is to control flows of resources rather than the stock and extraction of resources.

Consequently, the trading companies' ownership is characterised by minority ownership (most frequently less than 29 per cent interest), and it is in fact not rare that a nominal equity participation of less than one per cent is adopted in resource development ventures. Concomitantly, they often extend direct overseas loans on a concessionary basis in exchange for long-term supply contracts -- again to secure stable flows of resources.

Chapter VI

OVERSEAS SERVICE VENTURES

As could be expected from the diversity of business activities in which the general trading companies are engaged, their overseas ventures are not restricted to commerce, manufacturing and resource development. They also cover a variety of non-commerce, service-oriented businesses, which can be classified into the following seven categories: plant-export supportive ventures, such as construction, engineering, maintenance, and consulting; warehousing (including loading and unloading facilities); shipping and ship chartering; banking, finance and insurance; real estate; hotels and golf courses; and lastly, other services (which include printing, leasing, market research, restaurant management, etc.).

PLANT-EXPORT SUPPORTIVE VENTURES

In recent years, Japan has been remarkably successful in exporting high value-added capital goods -- for example, industrial plants producing electric power, steel, aluminium, fertilizers or petrochemicals, among others. Two-thirds of such exports are sold to developing countries and about one-fifth to communist countries. In 1970 Japan ranked fifth as a plant exporter among the OECD countries, after West Germany, the United States, the United Kingdom and France, but during the second half of the 1970s, it overtook the United Kingdom and France. And it is about to capture the lion's share of the world market for plant exports. Industrial plants are now one of Japan's major exports, accounting for about 10 per cent of total value (40).

There are certainly many factors that have contributed to this success. Perhaps the most significant is the fact that following World War II, Japanese industry restructured and upgraded its activities towards more sophisticated heavy and chemical industries. In so doing, the capital goods industry accumulated many skills and a good deal of experience in introducing improved plant layouts, machinery and equipment. This continuous rejuvenation of capital stock has been, in fact, an important source of Japan's productivity growth. And these experiences are embodied in the capital goods, and particularly plants, that Japanese industry now produces and exports.

Third World countries, eager to learn from Japan's recent experience of industrialisation, find this particularly attractive. Plant exports are a

erived demand either for industrialisation in developing countries or for
egional development in advanced countries. To compete with other manufac-
urers, information about new development projects must be gleaned as quickly
s possible. It is precisely because ot their global network of intormation
hat the trading companies are credited with Japan's success in plant exports,
ince they are in an excellent position to assist plant manufacturers in
nformation-gathering, financing and plant installation. Indeed, the majority
r Japan's plant exports are either directly contracted or indirectly assisted
y trading companies. Mitsui, Mitsubishi, C. Itoh, ana Marubeni have been the
eaaing plant exporters, although Nissho Iwai has performea exceptionally well
n recent years, joining the leading pack (see Annex 2 Table 8).

As might be expectea, each traaing company tends to tie up with plant
anufacturers and engineering companies within its own industrial group
- this tendency is perhaps most pronounced with Mitsubishi and Sumitomo --
hough group attiliation is not an unbreakable rule. Depending upon the cir-
umstances, flexible pragmatic tie-ups are made between the trading companies
nd manutacturers or engineering companies ot different groups, as well as
mong the trading companies themselves.

Many of these plant exports are made frequently on a turnkey basis.
ndeed, turnkey contracts can be comprehensive enough to include construction
f infrastructure -- for example port and surtace transportation facilities --
s well as plant installation and training of local plant managers and opera-
ives. The more complex the technological components, the more comprehensive
he services rendered and the more often such services are demandea, particu-
arly when the plant is purchasea by a developing country. Construction, en-
ineering, maintenance and consulting ventures set up overseas are designed to
rovide some ot these services.

Once again, joint ventures involving the participation of local inte-
ests (types C and D) are the most commonly adopted. They reflect the efforts
ade by trading companies not only to enhance their competitiveness but also
o facilitate transfers ot skills to local interests. In fact, in many cases
hey were established at the specific request of the host government (41).

The traaing companies are on the whole minority owners of these sup-
ortive ventures tor plant exports. Yet when other Japanese investors, like
anufacturers or engineering firms, are included, there is nearly the same
umber ot majority ana minority-owned ventures. These joint investors are
deally suited to provide the necessary technical services, which local inte-
ests, particularly in developing countries, usually cannot. Moreover, tech-
ical requirements, and particularly delivery schedules, are such that ma-
ority control is otten neeaed for these supportive ventures.

Practically all these ventures -- 36 out ot a total ot 39 -- are in
eveloping countries. So far, Brazil is the only Latin American country where
his type of investment is made. In Asia, several countries -- Indonesia,
outh Korea, the Philippines, Singapore and Thailand -- host these invest-
ents, which are as yet limited in number. Oil-producing Arab countries,
otably Saudi Arabia ana Kuwait, are another group ot host countries. They
re all important customers for Japan's plant exports.

Recently some developing countries burdened with heavy external debts
ave been asking plant exporters to make leasing arrangements instead of

outright export sales. The big trading companies, which have gained experi
ence in the leasing of aircraft, ships and computers are adapting to this ne
development. Mitsubishi Corporation, for example, has set up a special tas
force to cope with such requests from the developing countries and has create
a new leasing company. Other leading traders are taking similar steps. A
the time of writing, the export of a synthetic textile mill to Indonesi
(negotiated by Mitsui and Mitsubishi) and a power station to the Philippine
(negotiated by Nissho Iwai), both under leasing arrangements, are said to b
in the making.

WAREHOUSING FACILITIES

Warehousing naturally plays a critical role in a chain of distributio
channels -- from one geographical point to another or from a spot market to
future market. There is, however, no need for trading companies to directl
own and operate warehouses. They can either lease them under a long-ter
contract or deal with independent warehousing firms. Leasing or consignmen
is probably more economical and more flexible than direct ownership, parti
cularly when flows of goods to be intermediated are neither large enoug
(hence, warehouses are too costly to own) nor last long enough. As a result
the number of warehouses owned abroad by the nine trading companies is stil
small (23 in 1980), although there are some signs of increased interest i
-- and an increased need for -- such facilities in connection with their over
seas resource development ventures.

Although these warehousing ventures exhibit a somewhat disperse
pattern of types of investment, there is an indication of the trading com
panies' willingness (or perhaps need) to form joint ventures with loca
interests (42).

Thirteen of the trading companies' 23 warehousing ventures are locate
in developing countries, where they are often set up because the needed faci
lities are simply not available (e.g., storing facilities for chemicals). O
the other hand, they are established in advanced countries (especially th
United States, Canada and Australia) when resources exported to Japan (such a
coal and iron ore) or manufactures exported from Japan (such as cars) are sub
stantial in quantity and continuous in transaction.

As far as the ownership pattern is concerned, minority ownership i
nearly as frequent as majority ownership if the group shares of Japanes
interests are taken into account. If, however, only the shares of the tradin
companies themselves are taken into account, they are more frequently minorit
rather than majority-owned.

SHIPPING

Like warehousing, shipping (including ship chartering), is of logisti
importance to trading companies. As the volume of trade rose, they began t
set up their own shipping ventures: practically all of them were establishe

after 1970, and especially in the second half of the 1970s. Mitsubishi and C. Itoh are the two most active firms in shipping ventures (11 and 19 ventures, respectively, in 1980), followed by Mitsui with nine and Tomen with seven.

The most common form of investment, 100 per cent ownership by the home office (Type A), can be explained by the rather unique conditions afforded shipping ventures. Many of them are merely "dummy" corporations set up in tax havens like Bermuda, Panama or Liberia, that offer advantages for ship registration. These establishments for "flags of convenience" are wholly-owned (wholly-manipulated) operations, which is reflected in ownership patterns.

When joint ventures are formed, the trading companies choose as their co-investors independent shipping companies, many of which are member companies of their affiliated industrial groups at home. For the moment, these shipping ventures are not competitive but rather supplement the services offered by independent shipping companies (43).

BANKING, FINANCE AND INSURANCE

The nine trading companies' overseas ventures in banking, finance (in the form of holding companies) and insurance numbered 36 in 1980. They are concentrated mostly in advanced countries, especially the United States, Canada and Australia. Only a limited number of developing economies, such as Hong Kong, Singapore and Bermuda, are hosting this type of venture. Mitsui, Mitsubishi, C. Itoh, Marubeni, Sumitomo and Tomen are relatively active investors in finance-related ventures.

Their reason for investing in banking has been primarily to "keep the banks company". When their transacting banks happened to advance overseas, the trading companies decided to co-operate, for they had often set up operations in certain foreign locations much earlier than the banks. Their investment shares are very nominal, ranging from less than 1 per cent to about 4 per cent, and the number of investments is also limited (nine cases in 1980).

Though Japanese banks may have needed the trading companies' co-operation as joint investors, in the early days of their overseas advance, they are now investing independently or in collaboration with one another. Indeed, they have on occasion been in rivalry with the trading companies, for they themselves are increasingly interested in playing the role of project financier for overseas ventures.

For their part, the trading companies may no longer be as eager to expand their banking activity by way of direct capital participation. After the fall of the Shah, for example, the International Bank of Iran and Japan, set up in Teheran in 1959 with 32 per cent Japanese interest (the Bank of Tokyo, Mitsubishi Corporation, C. Itoh, Tomen, and five other companies) was immediately expropriated. The trading companies may perhaps continue to participate on a "companionship" basis if, for some compelling reason, they are called upon to collaborate with the banks, but this will most likely be only token participation.

67

On the other hand, the trading companies are somewhat more active in joining local investment finance companies as minority shareholders or tying up with their industrial group members to establish new investment finance companies. These ventures are specialised in a particular industrial sector in a given locality (44).

But the trading companies' investments in these holding companies are at the moment limited in number (22 instances in 1980) and are aimed more at resource-extractive ventures than at manufacturing. Their capital participation in local companies is also quite nominal, usually less than 10 per cent, although it is somewhat higher when they collaborate with Japanese interests in setting up new investment ventures overseas.

There also exist a handful of insurance ventures set up by trading companies, but they are in fact more like insurance agents operating with a small staff and a limited amount of capital.

REAL ESTATE

The trading companies' overseas ventures in real estate involve both commercial (office buildings) and residential properties. Many of the commercial property ventures set up by trading companies originated with the expansion of their branch offices abroad.

They began by renting office space, but as such facilities are often in short supply, especially in the developing countries, they went on to build or purchase their own office buildings. It was a logical step to move into the office rental business for whatever extra space was available. This was the case for the many office buildings owned and managed by Mitsui, Sumitomo, and Marubeni (45).

These office buildings are usually occupied not only by the trading companies' respective overseas branch offices but also by those overseas ventures either established by the trading companies or closely affiliated with them. In other words, these real estate ventures were created in response to the demand for office space derived mainly from the trading companies' own overseas operations.

In the area of residential properties, some ventures are engaged in comprehensive housing development projects in advanced countries, while others are involved in the brokerage business, intermediating the sales of local properties. In the latter type of venture, the amount of capital invested is usually small: one such venture (wholly-owned) involves as little as $400 000.

These real estate ventures are mostly located either in rapidly developing countries (14 cases in Brazil and East Asian countries in 1980) where property values are expected to appreciate considerably or in North America (seven cases in the United States and Canada) where property values are relatively low by international -- and particularly Japanese -- standards. So far as ownership pattern is concerned, there seems to be a slight preference for majority ownership.

The trading companies' real estate investments are not limited to residential ventures, but also involve construction and management of hotels, golf courses and other associated recreational facilities.

HOTELS AND GOLF COURSES

The Japanese are among the world's most fervent globe trotters, both as businessmen and as tourists. Thanks to a sharp rise in personal income, coupled with the rise in value of the yen and the complete liberalisation of foreign exchange controls in the early 1970s, the demand for overseas travel expanded phenomenally, creating a variety of profitable business opportunities. The Japanese, especially businessmen, are also ardent golf lovers, and the Japanese brand of business entertainment often includes inviting clients for a game of golf. But because of land limitations at home, golf is a fairly expensive sport to play in Japan. It is therefore very common for business clients to be invited to spend, say a weekend, overseas for golf and travel.

The nine trading companies' investments in hotels and golf courses (14 cases in 1980) are at the moment concentrated in the United States and in Asian countries (South Korea, Hong Kong, Indonesia and the Philippines), though the traders themselves remain by and large minority shareholders (46).

OTHER SERVICE VENTURES

Another field of service venture is printing, in which trading companies are participating as minority co-investors. They are all located in developing countries where a large number of Japanese companies, including the traders themselves, have local operations. In this way the companies are assured of a sufficiently large demand for printing services. Japan's two leading printing companies, Dai Nippon and Toppan, are taking advantage of this new market by setting up shop in collaboration with both trading companies and local interests. (These are all type D ventures.)

Dai Nippon, for instance, is in partnership with Mitsubishi Corporation and local interests -- two in Singapore and one in Malaysia. It also operates in partnership with Sumitomo Corporation and local interests in Indonesia. Japanese interests in these ventures range from 30 to 51 per cent. Toppan also operates two such ventures, one in Indonesia with C. Itoh (20 per cent interest) and local interests (50 per cent), and another in Singapore with Mitsui & Co. (7.98 per cent interest) and local interests (8.51 per cent).

The trading companies are also involved in leasing ventures of, for example, capital goods, such as small airplanes, containers in which to transport machinery, and construction equipment. Their customers are usually the trading companies' closely affiliated business firms rather than "open-market" clients. For example, trading companies often get into the leasing business to help client firms that need to use small planes for business trips. Perhaps because of the "closed" nature of their market, these leasing ventures are either wholly-owned or majority-owned by the traders themselves or in joint venture with other Japanese interests. Moreover, they are located in only a limited number of countries, including Singapore, Indonesia, the Philippines, Panama and the United States. At the moment there are less than ten leasing companies and they all operate with a small amount of paid-in capital ($5 million or less).

Other ventures include restaurants (mostly Japanese), financial consulting, market research and service agents for overseas ventures, each of which is quite limited in capitalisation and scope of operation. They are mostly auxiliary ventures derived from -- and supportive of -- the trading companies' own overseas investments in sales networks, manufacturing and resource extraction.

ASSESSMENT

The trading companies' investments are diverse in non-trade service sectors but are "capital-shallow" and quite small in scale of operation. Their primary goal is not so much to secure dividends per se but either to provide the necessary back-up services for their major lines of business or to "keep company" with their business clients for the sake of expanding as wide a network of affiliation as possible.

Ownership patterns vary with the nature of the operation. When the business is predominantly internal or "closed", as in shipping and real estate, these ventures are likely to be wholly or majority owned. In other cases, however, there is still a strong propensity for trading companies to remain minority shareholders.

It is worth stressing again that these overseas ventures in non-trade services should be regarded as business infrastructures. Although they may seem to be rather dispersed, incongruous and even unorganised, they do constitute the essential service elements strategically laid out to create each trading company's domain of overseas trade and investment activities. These motley services are indeed indispensable if transactional intermediation is to be carried out effectively. They are evidence of the trading companies' operations as infrastructural builders, particularly in developing countries, where business infrastructure is lacking.

Chapter VII

IMPLICATIONS FOR DEVELOPING COUNTRIES

There is an ironical twist to the general trading companies' performance as multinationals: the more extensive and successful their overseas operations, the stronger the motivation of developing host countries to create their own trading companies patterned after the Japanese model. Perhaps too, the more restrictive are the measures some host governments impose on Japanese trading companies in their effort to foster their own -- the Republic of Korea, for example, has prohibited the establishment of wholly-owned trading subsidiaries by Japan's trading companies.

It is also true that in many developing countries there is a deep-rooted suspicion of middlemen. Local traders have long been considered as parasitic exploiters of producers, and particularly of farmers and cottage-industry workers. Today, however, the Japanese-type general trading companies are being recognised as something "new" that can contribute positively to national welfare. In developing countries they are being seen as an effective vehicle for industrialisation.

This change of attitude is based in part on the realisation that the full benefits of international trade cannot be reaped unless the developing countries themselves are able to handle the marketing of their own exports and the procurement of their own imports (47).

It is important to remember that when Japan was opened to international trade in the mid-19th century, it quickly recognised that its lack of preparation was a source of commercial inequality and therefore set out to foster its own trading companies to replace foreign traders in intermediating Japan's exports and imports. This import substitution in commerce was carried out at a time when industrial groups (the zaibatsu) were being formed. Within each group, one trading company was granted the exclusive right to intermediate group-related trade. Following World War II, the zaibatsu were dissolved and newly structured industrial groups emerged. However, to this day, the trading companies continue to operate with their closely affiliated groups as the home base. The net result has been the emergence of unique mercantile institutions whose performance and efficiency in both intermediating trade and organising overseas ventures are unrivalled in the world. Japan has thus turned its original disadvantage into one of its trump cards for trade and investment. The historical experience of Japan can no doubt serve as a valuable lesson for today's developing countries.

In the preceding chapters we examined in detail the Top Nine trading companies' ventures around the world. These investment activities -- and strategies -- must constantly be adapted to a changing business environment both at home and abroad. At this juncture, let us recapitulate our findings about their overseas involvement and consider further implications for developing host countries.

In the early postwar years Japan's trading companies quickly re-established their worldwide outposts to export home-made products as well as to secure the vital overseas supplies of capital goods, industrial materials, fuels and foodstuffs Japan lacked at home. Indeed, they created a great diversity of entrepreneurial activities and a variety of new forms of investment by which they set up and co-ordinate overseas ventures. In the commercial sector, which is the principal area of their operations, the trading companies have woven a far-flung network of sales and procurement organisations either alone or in close collaboration with a multitude of different business interests in practically every nook and cranny of the world's commercial regions. With their increased involvement in overseas direct investments in the non-commercial sector (manufacturing, resource development and non-trade services), the companies' trading outposts have been gradually integrated into a scheme of multinational operations. In fact, the major regional offices are now encouraged to become "independent" and "indigenised", with greater emphasis on both local and third-country trade intermediation than on Japan-linked business operations, although the latter still constitute the bulk of their business.

The trading companies' endeavour to generate third-country or offshore trade business is in part being forced on them by developing countries that impose counter-purchase requirements on imports. Similarly, the Communist countries very frequently demand barter trade, forcing foreign exporters to accept local products in return. This type of compulsory reciprocal trade is often tied in with expensive plant imports, which frequently leave a big hole in the foreign-exchange coffers of developing countries. This "new" form of trade is thus closely interfaced with a "new" form of investment, turnkey plants. Compared with other countries, Japan is fortunate in this regard because its trading companies are relatively well prepared and capable of handling counter trade through their global network of information-gathering and marketing.

The trading companies' investments in the manufacturing sector, which are concentrated in developing countries, unequivocally show a high incidence of two "new" forms of investment: minority ownership and direct overseas loans. As we saw in Chapter IV, minority ownership (that is, equity participation of less than 50 per cent) is the most frequent mode of ownership (approximately 90 per cent of all cases). Equity participation of even less than 29 per cent still accounts for about 75 per cent of the nine trading companies' manufacturing ventures overseas. Why this high incidence of minority ownership? And does it imply more managerial control for local partners in the developing host countries?

The trading companies have a high propensity to be minority share-holders for, in the first place, they are basically incapable of running manu-facturing ventures by themselves (with a few exceptions involving simple manu-facturing operations). Their _primary_ business is trade intermediation, that is, they operate as commission brokers in the sphere of exchange and not in the sphere of production. Hence their equity participation in manufacturing ventures is kept at a minimum. They invest only to the extent that they can "capture" the trade opportunities created by such overseas ventures -- for example, those related to the installation of plants, machinery and equipment, the supply of raw materials and other inputs, and the marketing of outputs. The more exclusive domains they create for intermediation, the greater the volume of their business. Therefore, the trading companies try to create as many exclusive domains as possible by setting up affiliated ventures but minimise the amount of capital tied up in each venture as equity investment. In short, the trading companies are interested not so much in the ownership of production per se but in the control of transactional flows that can be derived from the operations of overseas ventures. Minority ownership is usually sufficient for this purpose. Simultaneously, trading companies can satisfy local demand for joint ventures in the developing host countries.

However, this does not mean that the trading companies neglect their equity investments. They are certainly interested in profitable investments as well; after all, the more profitable the venture, the greater the amount of dividends they receive -- and the greater the opportunities for transactional intermediation.

The trading companies also extend direct loans to their own manufacturing ventures overseas, particularly in developing countries, and the amounts of such loans can often exceed those of equity capital invested. This arrangement in part reflects their role as quasi-bankers and in part their preference for keeping investments as "liquid" as possible, so as to maintain a high rate of turnover on the use of capital. Such loans are often requested by local partners, who are unable to secure capital for their own share of equity ownership.

Direct overseas loans lie somewhere in between direct foreign investment (ownership and control) and portfolio investment (made solely for the purpose of capitalising on higher interest rates in the foreign financial markets). The direct loans arranged by trading companies are borrower-specific and entail an added degree of control of the debtor manufacturing companies, which are usually partially owned by the traders themselves. Unlike portfolio investments, they are not control-free loans and are much closer to direct foreign investment. As they are used by the trading companies for their manufacturing ventures, particularly in developing countries, these loans certainly deserve to be called a "new" form of investment, even though they have been common practice in their business operations at home.

Thus minority ownership does not necessarily mean that the trading companies have lost control. In this regard, the following observation of their investments in Indonesia deserves attention:

"The Japanese and the Australian Governments in particular both encourage their firms to enter into joint venture arrangements; however, despite these advantages, this arrangement of itself will not ensure smooth operations...

"The absence of a domestic medium- and long-term capital market has proven a barrier to the national partner as it forces him to take a minority snare in the joint venture. To illustrate this situation we can imagine a project in which total investment is set at US $20 million. Such a sum would normally comprise 30 per cent, i.e. US $6 million equity capital with the balance of 70 per cent coming from loans to the venture. In such a case even 20 per cent participation could well be beyond the capability of the domestic investor particularly if such a contribution must be paid in cash. More commonly a contribution of inputs such as land will be made with the balance being supplied by an additional loan finance equity payment thereby requiring that the share of the Indonesian partner be given as collateral to the foreign partner. In some cases a minor percentage will be given as free-shares to the national partner.

"With such an arrangement the outcome is obvious, dominant control of the enterprise by the foreign partner with all decisions on machinery, equipment, raw materials, manpower, management, marketing and product design being firmly vested in their hand" (48).

Thus, despite golden opportunities to participate in new ventures as equal partners, local investors remain in a state of dependency, not only because of financial weakness at the level of individuals but also because of an inadequate financial infrastructure at the national level. The same thing can be said of other infrastructural services, such as insurance, shipping, warehousing and consulting. The trading companies usually find it necessary -- and often profitable -- to invest in business infrastructures as a support for their principal ventures, say in manufacturing or resource development, simply because such facilities are not available in developing countries. Service ventures, however, are relatively small in scale and, as they are generally related to a given major venture, the spill-over effect (externalities to local communities) remains minimal.

The emergence of these service ventures does have the merit of pinpointing specific infrastructural deficiencies, to which the developing host countries should be alerted. There is definitely a need for host governments to promote not only physical (e.g., irrigation and communications) and social (e.g., education and health) infrastructures, but business infrastructures as well.

A VARIETY OF OTHER "NEW" FEATURES

The trading companies' manufacturing ventures present a few other "new" features, if not exactly "new" forms of investment. As we have seen, these ventures are concentrated in developing countries and are mostly centred around technologically standardized, labour-intensive industries: they are also relatively small in scale of operation. This set of characteristics is "new", in the sense that it contrasts sharply with the traditional, Western type of direct foreign investment, which is characterised by large-scale, capital-intensive and research-and-development-based manufacturing activities.

Second, by their choice of particular manufacturers as investment partners, the Japanese traders also implicitly choose particular product and process technologies. In this light, the trading companies can be seen as brokers for the transfer of labour-using technologies to developing countries, an aspect of their overseas operations that can also be considered a "new" or unconventional feature.

74

Third, the big trading companies are assisting some developing countries in setting up large-scale resource-based manufacturing ventures like
petrochemicals, projects that receive both financial and diplomatic support
from the Japanese Government as part of its international co-operation programme. These projects are usually not only carried out on a turnkey basis
-- a "new" form of investment -- but are also promoted by the Japanese
government as a substitute for military assistance (that is, arms exports), a
form of assistance on which there are serious constitutional constraints in
Japan but which other industrialised countries are all actively offering.
This feature, too, can be regarded as "new" -- at the least a peculiarity of
Japanese diplomacy.

Many of the "new" characteristics identified above can also be observed
in the trading companies' resource-development investments. Like manufacturing ventures, the 10 to 29 per cent range of minority ownership is the most
frequent, and less than 50 per cent equity participation accounts for 76 per
cent of all investments. In some instances minority ownership is so small
that it represents less than 1 per cent. Direct overseas loans are also
extensively used in the resource sector. They are extended not only to joint
ventures in which the traders participate but also to independent foreign
resource-producers in exchange for stable supply contracts. The trading companies are also actively involved, either as project organisers or participants, in large-scale resource development projects abroad in connection with
Japan's economic co-operation programme. Here, the fact that Japanese
industry and the government join efforts to secure stable supplies of overseas
resources -- Japan's well known "resource diplomacy" -- should again be recognised as a "new" pattern of investment.

Another "new" feature is cropping up in conjunction with Japan's plant
exports, for which the trading companies act as promoters. Some developing
countries, hard pressed for foreign exchange, are asking plant exporters to
convert purchase contracts into leasing arrangements. Since turnkey plant
operations are already classified as a "new form", this arrangement becomes,
so to speak, doubly new.

A QUASI-MARKET SYSTEM OF CO-OPERATION

As far as auxiliary trade and non-trade overseas ventures are concerned, then, Japan's general trading companies are engaged in a multitude of
"new" forms of overseas investment and rarely in the "old" form of wholly-
owned operation. Their investment approach is systems-focussed, that is, it
aims to create "closed" markets in which they can enjoy exclusive trading
opportunities. With the use of overseas investments -- both equity participation and direct loans -- the trading companies manoeuvre to inject elements
of imperfection into the market-place, yet without causing total market
failures or disruptions. On the contrary, they do create and expand markets
that did not exist before. But these markets are exclusively controlled not
by means of organisational internalisation (this is, controlled within the
firm) but by closely-knit, long-term collaboration with semi-autonomous business units (partially owned by and/or in debt to the trading companies).

At the core of this quasi-market system of co-operation and affiliation

are the trading companies' major offices, namely, their home and region.
headquarters. These central units are either wholly-owned or at lea
majority-owned to capture and retain control of commercial information, t
only firm-specific asset they possess, if only temporarily, before othe
sooner or later gain access to this "public good". Thus the "old" form
investment is still at the heart of their operations. But when their syst
of operations is looked at as a whole, it becomes apparent that a variety
"new" forms of investment are strategically deployed to generate busines
opportunities for intermediation.

After all, transactional intermediation still remains the prima
business -- and the primary source of income -- of the trading companies, a
this despite -- or rather, because of -- their recently acquired position
Japan's leading overseas investors.

Annex 1

INVESTMENT THEORY IN THE LIGHT OF THE
TRADERS' OVERSEAS ACTIVITIES

D. H. Robertson's famous phrase describing business organisations as "islands of conscious power in an ocean of unconscious operation" (49) has been used by other economists to help set up a theory of the firm. R. H. Coase used it first in explaining the existence of the firm in the market-place (50). Later, Stephen Hymer referred to it when he distinguished between the intra-firm hierarchical division of labour (co-ordinated by entrepreneurial decisions) and the inter-firm market co-ordinated division of labour (regulated by the price mechanism) with specific reference to the emergence of multinational corporations (51). Hymer presented his analysis as an extension of industrial organisation theory and not specifically as a theory of internalising a market.

It was in fact the Reading (UK) group of economists, led by John H. Dunning, that established the theory of market internalisation as the most useful paradigm to put the multinational operations of modern corporations into perspective. It was comprehensive enough to encompass all the monopolisitc theories of direct foreign investment developed till then by American economists, such as the industrial organisation theory (Hymer 1960, Kindleberger 1969, Caves 1971); the product cycle theory (Vernon 1966); the monetary account (Aliber 1970); the appropriability theory (Magee 1977); and the risk-diversification theory (Grubel 1968, Rugman 1979, Agmon and Lessard 1977) (52).

The Reading school gives two versions of "general" theory: the theory of internalising an intermediate-product market, expounded by Peter Buckley and Mark Casson and elaborated on by Casson (53), and the eclectic theory, introduced by John H. Dunning (54). Although the latter is more comprehensive in its coverage of explanatory factors than the former, internalisation is the central theme of both.

Buckley and Casson contend that all the "monopolistic advantages" theories can be synthesised with, and treated as special explanations of, theory of market internalisation. Their theory is built on three basic propositions:

1. Firms maximise profit in a world of imperfect markets.

2. When markets in intermediate products are imperfect, there is an incentive to bypass them by creating internal markets. This involves bringing under common ownership and control the activities that are linked by the market.

3. Internalisation of market across national boundaries generates MNEs (Multinational Enterprises) (55).

In addition, the Buckley and Casson model focusses on industry-specific factors. "These factors", they explain, "suggest particularly strong reasons for internalising markets for intermediate products in certain multistage production processes, and for internalising markets in knowledge. The first type of internalisation leads to the integration of production, marketing and R&D" (56). In all the different versions of the monopolistic theory of direct foreign investment, the core of the theory is that if the investing firm is to be successful, it must possess some innate advantages unavailable to local firms. It must compensate for the disadvantages of being away from home and of operating in a foreign market, namely the costs of acquiring local information and of communicating over long distances with headquarters in the home country. Yet all these theories, Buckley and Casson contend, provide no detailed explanation of how the advantages are generated in the first place. They appear as "manna from Heaven".

"In contrast," they write, "our theory provides a much more accurate and precise account of the origin of the attribute, or set of attributes, that give the MNE its advantages. We regard such advantages as the rewards for past investment in (i) R and D facilities which create an advantage in technological fields, (ii) the creation of an integrated team of skills, the rent from which is greater than the sum of the rewards to individuals, and therefore accruing to 'the firm' and within which individuals, as such, are dispensable, (iii) the creation of an information transmission network which allows the benefits of (i) and (ii) to be transmitted at low cost within the organisation, but also protects such information, including knowledge of market conditions, from outsiders." (57).

The eclectic approach, on the other hand, goes a step further by taking into account what Dunning calls "location-specific" factors that not only produce ownership-specific advantages but also assist (or hinder) the internalisation of such advantages when they are exploited in overseas markets. According to this theory, a firm will engage in foreign direct investment: (i) if it possesses ownership advantages (which are specific to the firm at least in the early stages of commercial exploitation); (ii) if it is more profitable for the firm "to internalise its advantages through an extension of its own activities rather than externalise them through licensing and similar contracts with independent firms"; and (iii) if the profitability of such internalisation rests on the utilisation of "at least some factor inputs (including natural resources) outside its home country" (58).

As Dunning summarizes it, "The greater the ownership advantages of enterprises ..., the more the incentive they have to exploit these themselves. The more the economics of production and marketing favour a foreign location, the more they are likely to engage in foreign direct investment. The propensity of a particular <u>country</u> to engage in international production is then dependent on the extent to which its enterprises possess these advantages and the locational attractions of its endowments compared with those offered by other countries" (59).

In short, the centrepiece of the Reading school's thought is the Robertson-Coasian concept of internalising a market by organisational direction and control. Direct foreign investment is interpreted as the phenomenon of market internalisation.

CO-OPERATION AND AFFILIATION: A LOOSE INTEGRATION

It is important to realise that the Robertson-Coasian dichotomy between firm and market, between hierarchical co-ordination and unconscious operation, does not take into account another important and very prevalent mode of organising industry and co-ordinating resource allocation, namely, the type of inter-firm co-operation and affiliation that enables individual firms to match ex ante, one another's plans.

This significant point was brought out by G. B. Richardson. "I was once", he writes, "in the habit of telling pupils that firms might be envisaged as islands of planned co-ordination in a sea of market relations. This now seems to me a highly misleading account of the way in which industry is in fact organised ... I imagine that this account of things might be acceptable, as a harmless first approximation, to a large number of economists. And yet there are two aspects of it that should trouble us. In the first place it raises a question, properly central to any theory of economic organisation, which it does not answer; and, secondly, it ignores the existence of a whole species of industrial activity which, on the face of it, is relevant to the manner in which co-ordination is achieved ... What I have in mind is the dense network of co-operation and affiliation by which firms are inter-related" (60).

The message is clear. When we focus on industry and the way in which it is organised, instead of on the individual firm or on the abstract notion of the market-place in general, we need still another concept, one that explains co-ordinating activities between the individual firms that comprise a given industry. It is true that the essence of the market is spontaneous co-ordination, while the essence of the firm is conscious planning. But the essence of industry is something else: it is the dense network of co-operation and affiliation.

This triple distinction is unambiguously stated by Richardson: "... the organisation of industry has ... to adapt itself to the fact that activities may be complementary. I shall say that activities are complementary when they represent different phases of a process of production and require in some way or another to be co-ordinated ...

"Now this co-ordination can be effected in three ways; by direction, by co-operation or through market transactions. Direction is employed when the activities are subject to a single control and fitted into one coherent plan ... Co-ordination is achieved through co-operation when two or more independent organisations agree to match their related plans in advance. The institutional counterparts to this form of co-ordination are the complex patterns of co-operation and affiliation which theoretical formulations too often tend to ignore. And, finally, co-ordination may come about spontaneously through market transactions ... as an indirect consequence of successive interacting decisions taken in response to changing profit opportunities" (61).

How then is this Richardsonian triple distinction relevant to our theory of corporate resource transfers across national borders? Is not hierarchical direction alone sufficient to describe the phenomenon of multinationalism? The answer, we contend, is unequivocally No. There is a wide range of international business activities that are carried out by co-operation and affiliation, but without total control by the intra-firm hierarchical decisions of a single multinational corporation. These activities include joint ventures, licensing, managerial and marketing contracts, turnkey projects, production sharing and other "new" forms of investment. Moreover, they are on the rise. In other words, co-operation is the increasingly popular mode of multinationalism, whereas internalisation is the mode less favoured by the host countries, notably in the Third World.

Furthermore, developing host countries are interested not in the growth of a particular multinational corporation in their markets but in the growth of their own domestic industry with the help of foreign capital and technology. What is relevant here is the organisation of industry and not the growth of an individual firm. Hence the establishment of industry through a network of co-operation and affiliation is the main concern of the host country. With this newly recognised mode of co-ordination in mind as the core of our analysis, let us now turn back to the trading companies and their group-investment activities.

TRADING COMPANIES AND "NEW" FORMS OF INVESTMENT

As our detailed examination in the preceding chapters shows, the trading companies' overseas investment activities present several features distinct from those shown by the traditional, "old" form of direct foreign investment: (1) a high propensity to form joint ventures; (2) a high incidence of minority ownership; (3) a very active use of direct overseas loans; (4) a significant involvement in turnkey projects of plant exports and, more recently, leasing arrangements for these plant facilities; (5) an active promotion of the transfers of labour-intensive, standardized (or "intermediate") technologies to developing countries; and (6) the provision of fairly comprehensive business infrastructures (e.g. financial, trading, warehousing, transport, and insurance services) for local business. All these features, which permeate the trading companies' networks of affiliated ventures, deserve to be recognised as "new" (or unconventional) forms of investment.

It is important to stress here that in their non-trade investment activities, trading companies normally do not prefer to -- and cannot -- internalise or replace markets, whereas internalisation is the key feature of the "old" form of investment. On the contrary, they endeavour to create new markets of their own in which they basically still profit as intermediaries, that is, markets that they can exploit by taking advantage of their affiliation and close involvement with other partners of overseas ventures.

By setting up overseas manufacturing ventures, for example, the trading company can earn commissions by securing investment-related capital goods, procuring necessary raw materials or intermediate inputs, and marketing finished products -- in addition to whatever dividends it may receive as a priority stockholder. Moreover, the trading company may earn interest on the direct loans it often extends to its overseas ventures. Dividends and interest are, however, almost incidental as a source of revenue.

Similarly, by organising and participating in resource-based, regional development projects, the trading company again secures the opportunity to earn commissions by acquiring and installing capital goods and by marketing extracted natural resources. Substantial commissions are likewise earned when it serves as the major contractor for comprehensive turnkey operations.

In short, trading companies strive to expand the domain of their intermediating (or brokerage) activities. They neither internalise hierarchically the new business opportunities nor leave them to pure-market, spontaneous co-ordination. The mode of co-ordination is definitely a loose integration accomplished by special associations with the parties involved. Trading companies have spun their own web of affiliated firms and conferred upon themselves, as it were, the privilege of intermediating trade for their associates on an exclusive-agent basis. This phenomenon may also be described as "market-like or quasi-market integration" as against "hierarchical intra-firm integration" (62).

We might add that co-ordination often cannot be left to hierarchical control by a single firm because the project involved and the range of economic activities associated with it is so huge that the cost of internalisation is prohibitive. This is often the case of regional development projects (i.e., there exists a natural barrier to internalisation). Another reason is that the host country often seeks to acquire corporate resources in unbundled form (that is, there exists a policy barrier to internalisation). However, in such situations, market-led spontaneous co-ordination can never be achieved either. Co-operation and association are thus the only realistic mode of co-ordination. And as we have seen, trading companies are structurally suited to operate under such conditions.

TRADING COMPANIES' INVESTMENT IN THEIR OWN COMMERCIAL FACILITIES

One important question still remains to be answered. How do trading companies obtain such unique ownership advantages as those entailed in the organiser/co-ordinator role? Unlike technology-based manufacturers, trading companies do not invest in research and development themselves; they do not generate knowledge internally. They gather both cross-sectional and inter-temporal information about supply and demand conditions in commodity markets (from raw materials and semi-processed goods to intermediate and finished products) as well as services (including technology). Once the information is obtained, it is "processed" into knowledge and becomes an ownership advantage for the trading companies. The more extensive the network of trading and marketing facilities, the easier and the more effective it is for them to collect information. Trading companies' ownership advantages are thus the fruit of their multinational operations. Herein lies their strength, which i quite unique.

Although John H. Dunning did not refer specifically to trading companies, he was the first to see the possibility of ownership advantages being created as a result of multinationality itself (63). He notes ways in which ownership advantages "specifically arise because of multinationality ... wider opportunities; more favoured access to and/or better knowledge about information, inputs, markets; ability to take advantage of international differences in factor endowments, markets; ability to diversify risks, e.g., in different currency areas" (64).

These descriptions, given as components of the eclectic theory, aptly fit the operations of trading companies.

This does not mean, however, that trading companies' activities can be adequately explained by the eclectic theory in its present form. Although Dunning's approach does take this important causal link between multinationality and ownership-specific advantages into account, his starting point is home-based ownership advantages, which may in turn be supplemented -- and reinforced -- by additional advantages accruing from multinationality, as clearly stated in the three sequential conditions explained earlier. In other words, multinationality-based advantages play only a supplementary and not a central role.

On the other hand, our theory of trading companies' involvement in international production begins with their multinational trade-intermediating operations (of the co-operative and affiliative type and not of the internalisation type), which give birth to ownership advantages that enable them to become effective organiser/co-ordinators of overseas ventures. Moreover, in exploiting such ownership advantages, trading companies are not interested in exercising intra-firm, hierarchical controls but resort to the Richardsonian mode of co-operation and association, the modus operandi not envisaged in the Coase-Robertson dichotomy between firm and market, hence left out of consideration in the eclectic theory.

The internalisation phenomenon itself, however, does apply to most of the overseas investments made by trading companies in their own global networks of branch offices and trading subsidiaries (such as Mitsubishi International, U.S.A.; Mitsui & Co., Europe S.A.; Sumitomo Corporation Italia, among others). Here the old form of investment -- whole ownership -- is pursued as the ideal form of investment for intelligence purposes, that is, collecting, exchanging, analysing and retaining information collected from a variety of markets, both at home and overseas. Internalisation of knowledge becomes crucial for their intelligence operations.

Yet there is a crucial difference between the internalisation efforts of trading companies and those of monopolistic manufacturers who have internally-generated advantages (such as patents). Entry is by far much easier for overseas investments in commerce than in manufacturing. Although the general trading companies are at present a feature unique to Japanese industry, rivalry can be exceedingly fierce, for a particular piece of valuable information acquired by one trading company may also become available to others, as such information is generated externally. Internalisation of knowledge is thus precarious at best. The market in which trading companies operate is no doubt highly competitive, and this is the very reason why they have to operate on very thin margins of commission (see Chapter II).

GROUP INVESTMENT AND THE PRINCIPLE OF COMPARATIVE ADVANTAGE

One of the distinctive features of Japanese overseas investment is the prevalence of group investments organised by trading companies, as seen in Japan's manufacturing investments in labour-intensive products as well as in its resource-oriented ventures abroad (which both involve its comparatively disadvantaged industries).

What makes Japanese industry adopt group investments? What facilitates and encourages such an approach? The industrial organisation of Japanese industry itself is undoubtedly responsible for this peculiarity. As we noted in Chapter II, each major trading company, as a key member of a particular keiretsu group, has well-established, closely-knit business relationships with a large number of companies, including banks, insurance companies and shipping firms. As we mentioned earlier, trading companies assist their own manufacturing subsidiaries and affiliates in relocating production overseas whenever their home-based production loses comparative advantage. This is a clear indication that the operations of trading companies are strongly governed by the doctrine of comparative costs (65).

Thanks to their long experience in dealing with a wide variety of products and simultaneously handling both exports and imports, the trading companies have developed a keen sense of comparative costs. They make buying and selling decisions with the international division of labour in mind as a matter of routine. This orientation is natural -- and in fact profitable -- for them, since they can create many more opportunities to earn commissions if they assist trading countries on the basis of comparative costs rather than of absolute advantage. When a trading company acts as the organiser of overseas ventures, the same principle is again applied, guiding such ventures along the lines of comparative advantage.

It was in fact the trading companies that were the first to detect a decline in Japan's comparative advantage in low-skilled, labour-intensive goods in the early 1960s and to urge Japanese manufacturers to establish overseas ventures in neighbouring Asian countries with lower wages and also to procure such goods there. It was also an association of trading companies, the Foreign Trade Council, that castigated the food-self-sufficiency programme proposed in 1975 by the Agricultural Policy Council, an advisory organ of the Ministry of Agriculture, Forestry and Fisheries. Agriculture in Japan is obviously a comparatively disadvantaged, inefficient industry and the trading companies, Japan's bastion of free trade, naturally objected.

Interestingly enough, trading companies also organise consortiums of companies (joint participants) within their affiliated keiretsu group under the principle of comparative advantage. Such arrangements are particularly suitable when an overseas venture is huge in scale and cost, as is the case of regional development projects. No single firm may be quite large or efficient enough to provide all the necessary functions (e.g., construction, installation of plants, equipment and machinery, financing, and marketing of extracted resources). Yet each firm does have a comparative advantage in performing a <u>particular</u> function (66).

Consequently, with the <u>intra-group</u> division of labour adopted by the participating firms, the efficiency -- hence the competitiveness -- of operations offered in a group-integrated package of services can be enhanced to a significant degree. Herein lies an important source of advantage for group investors to implement huge-scale overseas ventures. The relative weakness of individual firms is actually turned into an advantage. Indeed, whenever the trading company selects investment participants, it does so with the above principle in mind. In short, the principle of comparative advantage is <u>doubly</u> activated -- first at the organisational level of group investors and again at the locational level of the investment.

In terms of efficiency, <u>the group-integrated package of services</u> is clearly superior to <u>the intra-firm, internalised package of services</u>. Here it is important to distinguish between two types of scale economies: "genuine economies of scale" and "pseudo-economies of scale" (67). Genuine economies of scale are those that arise from the saving of real resources and the reduction of costs in production or in sales. They are beneficial to both private firms and society.

Pseudo-economies of scale, on the other hand, bring no benefit to society; though private benefits may increase, they actually increase social costs. The prime example is transfer pricing, which allows companies to evade taxes; this enlarges private profits at a cost to society. Pseudo-economies are also evident when multinationals are invited to operate in the host country's comparatively disadvantaged industries under tariff protections. In short, a group investment that is governed by the principle of comparative costs in both structure and direction is less susceptible to pseudo-economies than hierarchically integrated investments, even if it is not completely free from them.

TRANSACTIONAL INTERMEDIATION IN THE QUASI-MARKET

As transactional brokers, the trading companies' advantage lies in their knowledge of market conditions. Under what conditions do non-trader firms ask for the intermediary services that use such knowledge?

To satisfy their customers, trading companies must be able to reduce transactions costs (i.e., offer trader-specific marketing or procurement cost advantages) and/or provide a particular type of qualitative (non-price) marketing service required for a specialised line of product, such as technical and promotional services (i.e., offer product-specific non price marketing advantages). The first type of advantage, which can be realised both through scale economies in transaction and through specialised knowledge about a particular market, has traditionally been the traders' forte.

But the trading companies are also endeavouring to develop the second type of advantage. For example, in their efforts to intermediate in plant exports, they have hired a large number of engineers and set up a special sales force that can provide technical services. In the absence of these advantages, non-trader firms will use either pure market (i.e., direct market transactions without the intermediation of traders) or hierarchy (i.e., non-traders themselves set up marketing units within their own organisations). In other words, the "departure-from-trader" phenomenon will occur in either case.

In this connection, some of the transactional concepts emphasized by Oliver E. Williamson -- specifically, information impactedness, opportunism and atmosphere -- are quite useful for our discussion (68). He explains these three concepts as follows:

Information impactedness: "It exists when true underlying circumstances relevant to the transaction, or related set of transactions, are known to one or more parties but cannot be costlessly discerned by or displayed for others" (69).

Opportunism: "Opportunism extends the conventional assumption that economic agents are guided by considerations of self-interest to make allowance for strategic behaviour ... It is to be distinguished from both stewardship behaviour and instrumental behaviour. Whereas stewardship behaviour involves a trust relation in which the word of a party can be taken as his bond, instrumental behaviour is a more neutral mode in which there is no necessary self-awareness that the interests of a party can be furthered by strategems of any sort (I. Goffman, Strategic Interaction, 1969). Opportunistic behaviour differs from both because it involves making "false or empty, that is, self-disbelieved, threats and promises in the expectation that individual advantage will thereby be realised" (Goffman, p.105) (70).

Atmosphere: "Reference to atmosphere is intended to make allowance for attitudinal interactions and the systems consequences that are associated therewith" (71).

Williamson uses these concepts to examine under what conditions the market fails and will consequently be replaced by internal organisation. He is thus concerned with the two polar modalities of co-ordination: market vs. hierarchy. On the other hand, trading companies as intermediaries operate as entities in the interface between the two, strongly siding with the market rather than internal organisation. For when all transactions are internalised, there is no more business left for transactional brokers. So long as the market exists under conditions of uncertainty, opportunities always abound for intermediation.

In order to justify their existence, trading companies must necessarily possess some sort of market information that others do not have at a particular point in time and be willing to take risks in the face of uncertainties. Information impactedness is the sine qua non of their existence. Indeed, this concept further helps to explain their strategy of keeping their central and regional offices wholly-owned.

There is one important question raised by Williamson that is directly applicable to traders' business, that is, the question of opportunism. "... Suppose that the common information-collection responsibilities are assigned by contract to one of the parties. The purchasing party then runs a veracity risk: information may be filtered and possibly distorted to the advantage of the firm that has assumed the information-collection responsibility. If checks are costly and proof of contractual violation difficult, contractual sharing arrangements manifestly experience short-run limitations. If, in addition, small-numbers conditions prevail, so that options are restricted, contractual sharing is subject to long-run risks as well. On this argument integration for purposes of observational economies is again to be traded ultimately to transaction-cost considerations" (72).

Doesn't the responsibility for information-collection in their overseas joint ventures lead the trading companies to act in an opportunistic fashion? Do forces or institutional arrangements exist that attenuate the incentives for opportunism?

There seem to be several restraining factors. First, trading companies aim for mutually profitable, long-term relationships with other business interests. They are not fly-by-night operators. Their interest lies more in continuous transactions than in one-shot deals. They are always in search of linked business opportunities.

Second, trading companies are active, if partial, equity investors in local ventures. The costs of opportunism, if practised, will therefore have to be incurred by themselves.

Third, trading companies' advantages lie in the sphere of trade and not in the sphere of production. Their joint partners have advantages either in production or in local marketing, or both. Hence the possibility of opportunism is symmetrical: their joint partners, too, may act opportunistically. But if each party indulges in opportunism, the joint venture is bound to fail. There is therefore a strong incentive for each party to select its partners very cautiously so that a joint venture can be managed with mutual trust. Besides, the number of parties involved in a joint venture is usually so small that opportunistic behaviour is apt to be detected without much difficulty.

Given the above atmosphere in which both trust and policing exists, the incidence of opportunism (in the sense of a malicious act to realise self-interest by making "false or empty, that is, self-disbelieved, threats and promises") is likely to be rare, though the possibility always exists. Trading companies' overall behaviour probably corresponds better to the model of "stewardship behaviour" -- that is, "a trust relation in which the word of a party can be taken as his bond" (73). Stewardship behaviour is clearly required if trading companies are to succeed in playing the role of organiser/co-ordinator for large-scale ventures abroad.

TOWARD THE "INTERNATIONAL DIVISION-OF-LABOUR" THEORY OF INVESTMENT

The concept of market internalisation has recently gained currency as a paradigm for the theory of direct foreign investment (74). In the light of the preceding analysis, however, we feel that a call for the acceptance of internalisation as a general theory is premature.

The notion of internalisation describes only a single individual firm's effort to maximise its own monopolistic profits -- totally neglecting the interests of both the home and host economies. It is a concept appropriate only in microeconomic partial equilibrium analysis. Internalisation is the opposite extreme of spontaneous and unconscious co-ordination of the market mechanism. As our analysis has shown, there are, however, many instances of international production carried out through co-operation among several -- or even more -- closely affiliated parties rather than through a single firm's effort to internalise market opportunities hierarchically.

In fact, what has tentatively been identified as the "new" forms of investment (75) is nothing other than international resource transfers that can be realised only under the Richardsonian modus operandi of co-operation and loose integration. Internalisation applies to the old form of investment, that is, the wholly-owned operations of a single multinational corporation by means of which all essential (in many cases non-essential) corporate resources -- knowledge, capital, marketing facilities, etc. -- are transferred in a complete intra-firm package without leaving room for local interests to participate and learn from experience.

The most typical type of market imperfection or failure in developing countries can be traced to a lack of resources like those of modern corporations. Since the market itself fails to work, its famed invisible hand is non-existent. This leaves only two alternatives: hierarchical control or co-operative integration. A single large multinational may be able to take advantage of market imperfections if it possesses those missing resources; the firm then internalises markets, but often pseudo-economies of scale are involved.

Alternatively, the host country can remedy such market imperfections by acquiring the missing inputs through co-operative arrangements in unbundled form, such as licensing, managerial and marketing contracts, production sharing, joint ventures, turnkey operations, and other new forms of foreign investment. And this is exactly what many developing countries are endeavouring to do. In other words, what they aim at is the macro-economic success of building industry at home by acquiring key corporate resources in such a manner that these resources are fully assimilated and become part and parcel of the local factor endowments.

What is at issue here, then, is not the welfare of a single corporation but the welfare of the global economy. We are concerned with the issues of economic development -- development that can be assisted by corporate resource transfers -- and the impact of development on the international division of labour. We must move towards "an economic development theory" or "an international division of labour theory" of direct foreign investment. The task is not an easy one; but no doubt the first step is to recognise the Richardsonian triple distinction of international resource allocation and incorporate it into our analysis as a key theoretical element.

Table 1

PROFIT MARGINS OF NINE TRADING COMPANIES, 1968-1978
(in percentage*)

	1968	1973	1974	1975	1976	1977	1978
Mitsubishi	2.14	2.06	2.10	1.91	1.97	1.92	2.00
Mitsui	2.30	2.26	2.06	1.64	1.72	1.72	1.79
C. Itoh	2.16	2.71	1.92	1.78	1.93	1.86	1.91
Marubeni	2.40	2.84	2.36	2.16	2.22	1.92	2.07
Sumitomo	3.53	2.03	1.97	1.88	1.92	1.83	1.88
Nissho Iwai	2.35	2.38	2.33	2.14	2.15	1.95	2.14
Tohmen	2.44	3.05	2.80	2.50	2.37	2.37	2.21
Kanematsu	2.68	2.33	2.04	1.82	2.07	2.11	2.11
Nichimen Jitsugyo	1.96	2.82	2.28	2.50	2.55	2.55	2.63

* Gross sales profit margin = Gross profits ÷ Total sales

Source: Kyoikusha, idem., p. 173.

Table 2

EQUITY AND DEBT CAPITAL EXTENDED BY TOP NINE TRADING COMPANIES, 1978
(in millions of yen)

	A. Equity Investment at Home and Abroad		B. Loans (at Home and Abroad)		C. Total (A + B)		D. Rate of Return on Equity Investment	E. Overseas Financing (Equity and Loans as Percentage of C)*	
	Amount	%	Amount	%	Amount	%	%	Amount	%
Mitsubishi Corp.	177 955	38.6	283 361	61.4	461 316	100.0	9.4	140 200	30.4
Mitsui & Co.	283 536	39.0	443 056	61.0	726 582	100.0	3.1	248 700	34.2
C. Itoh & Co.	239 958	42.1	329 625	57.9	569 583	100.0	2.2	115 300	20.2
Marubeni Corp.	159 727	53.5	138 695	46.5	298 422	100.0	2.2	126 100	42.3
Sumitomo Corp.	109 554	63.8	62 053	36.2	171 607	100.0	2.0	59 300	34.6
Nissho Iwai	65 217	40.9	94 325	59.1	159 542	100.0	2.0	61 000	38.2
Tomen	42 376	43.3	55 457	56.7	97 853	100.0	2.0	41 700	42.6
Kanematsu Gosho	34 461	31.8	74 021	68.2	108 482	100.0	1.3	25 200	23.2
Nichimen Jitsugyo	24 538	33.2	49 319	66.8	73 857	100.0	1.2	29 600	40.1

The trading companies do not make public the breakdown between overseas equity investments and loans. One estimate made from their financial statements for fiscal 1980 (April 1, 1980 - March 30, 1981) puts the equity-debt ratio of overseas investment for Mitsubishi at 80 to 20; for Mitsui 65 to 35; for C. Itoh 82 to 18; for Marubeni 90 to 10; for Sumitomo 87 to 13; for Nissho Iwai 64 to 36; for Tomen 89 to 11; for Kanematsu Gosho 86 to 14; and Nichimen Jitsugyo 91 to 9. This, however, does not include offshore-arranged loans, which are known to be quite substantial in amount but for which no statistics are available. Hence the equity-debt ratios shown here are concerned only with financial flows made directly from Japan.

89

Table 3

COMMUNICATIONS EXPENDITURES OF THE TOP NINE, 1978
(in millions of Yen)

Trading Company	Communications expenditure	Communications expenses/ total sales expenses
Mitsubishi Corporation	4 337	3.04%
Mitsui & Co.	11 936 *	9.60% *
C. Itoh & Co.	3 528	3.87
Marubeni Corporation	3 593	3.78
Sumitomo Corporation	3 528	4.31
Nissho Iwai	3 386	4.68
Tomen	685 **	1.87 **
Kanematsu Gosho	1 494	4.47
Nichimen Jitsugyo	1 474	3.82

* Including computer expenses estimated at about 6 billion Yen
** Expenses incurred at headquarters only.

Source: Idem, p. 266

Table 4a

REGIONAL OVERSEAS HEADQUARTERS OF THE TOP NINE SUBSIDIARIES

	Mitsui	Mitsubishi	Marubeni	C. Itoh	Sumitomo	Nissho Iwai	Tomen	Kanematsu	Nichimen
U.S.A. (New York)	•	•	•	•	•	•	•	•	•
Canada (Toronto)	•	•	•	•	•	•	•	•	•
Argentina (Buenos Aires)	•	•	•	•	•	•		•	
Brazil (Sao Paulo)	•	•	•	•	•	•	•	•	
Chile (Santiago)		•							
Colombia									
Mexico (Mexico City)		•	•					•	
Panama (Panama)									
Peru (Lima)									
Venezuela (Caracas)									
W. Germany (Dusseldorf)	•	•	•*	•	•	•	•	•	•
France (Paris)	•	•	•*	•	•	•		•	
Belgium (Brussels)		•	•*		•				
Holland (Amsterdam or Rotterdam)									
Italy (Milan)			•**						
Spain (Madrid)			•**						
Portugal (Lisbon)									
Sweden (Stockholm)			•*						
U.K. (London)									
Greece (Athens)									
Hong Kong	•	•	•	•	•	•	•	•	•
Thailand (Bangkok)	•	•	•	•	•	•		•	•
Pakistan (Karachi)									
Australia (Sydney)	•	•	•	•	•	•	•	•	•
New Zealand (Auckland)	•	•	•					•	
Iran (Teheran)**	•	•		•	•	•	•	•	•

* These Marubeni offices are not wholly-owned. Participation in West Germany is 80 per cent, in Belgium 66 per cent, and in Italy, Spain and Sweden, 65 per cent.

** These offices were closed at the time of writing.

REGIONAL DISTRIBUTION OF AUXILIARY VENTURES IN COMMERCE
(by type*, 1980)

	A	B	C	D	A'	B'	C'	D'	Regional Total
Developing regions									71
Asia	4	1	11	22	0	0	2	7	47
Latin America	4	0	6	2	0	2	0	1	15
Middle East	0	0	1	2	0	0	0	0	3
Africa	0	0	4	1	0	0	0	1	6
Developed regions									174
North America	12	14	4	4	22	14	19	4	93
Europe	2	19	13	5	4	10	2	3	58
Oceania	1	1	1	8	1	4	4	3	23
Total by type	23	35	40	44	27	30	27	19	245

* Type A (or A'): Ventures wholly-owned by the home (or a regional) office of a trading company

  Type B (or B'): Joint ventures owned by the home (or a regional office of a trading company and a Japanese company or companies. They are wholly-owned by Japanese interests.

  Type C (or C'): Joint ventures between the home (or a regional) office of a trading company and local interests.

  Type D (or D'): Joint ventures among the home (or a regional) office of a trading company, a Japanese company or companies, and local interests (and/or third-country interests).

Table 4c

AUXILIARY TRADING VENTURES BY THE COMMODITY TRADED (1980)

	Mitsui	Mitsubishi	Marubeni	C. Itoh	Sumitomo	Nissho Iwai	Tomen	Kanematsu	Nichimen	Total Ventures Number	%
Agricultural, marine and forestry products	12	2	5	1	0	1	3	0	2	26	10.6
Minerals & fuels	2	0	1	1	0	1	2	0	0	7	2.9
General commerce	2	3	1	1	2	3	2	1	1	16	6.5
Manufactures											
food & beverages	4	0	0	0	0	0	1	1	0	6	2.4
textiles	6	1	5	6	0	0	3	1	3	25	10.2
metal products	6	4	2	2	4	2	2	0	0	22	9.0
motor cars, motorcycles and parts	5	3	8	9	5	1	1	0	1	33	13.5
Chemicals	2	1	0	0	0	1	0	1	0	5	2.0
Electrical machinery	0	17	4	3	0	0	2	1	1	28	11.4
Non-electric machinery	3	0	11	5	4	2	1	1	3	30	12.2
Other (sundries)	16	10	8	4	1	1	1	6	0	47	19.2
Total by company	58	41	45	32	16	12	18	12	11	245	100.0

Table 4d

OWNERSHIP INTEREST IN AUXILIARY TRADING VENTURES

Ownership and Interest	Mitsui	Mitsubishi	Marubeni	C. Itoh	Sumitomo	Nissho Iwai	Tomen	Kanematsu	Nichimen	Total Ventures Number	%
1 to 9%	5	10	5	2	1	3	1	0	1	28	11.4
10 to 29%	12	9	11	4	4	6	2	6	1	55	22.4
30 to 49%	10	15	10	8	4	3	5	1	3	59	24.1
50%	7	1	7	4	1	0	1	1	2	24	9.8
51 to 79%	5	1	2	3	2	0	3	3	1	20	8.2
80 to 100%	16	4	10	11	4	0	6	1	3	55	22.5
n.a.	3	1	0	0	0	1	0	1	0	4	1.6
Total	58	41	45	32	16	12	18	12	11	245	100.0

THIRD-COUNTRY TRADE BY TOP NINE TRADERS (BY VALUE, RATIO TO TOTAL SALES,
PROPORTION CARRIED OUT BY OVERSEAS OFFICES, 1978)
(In millions of Yen)

Trading Company	Value	Ratio to total sales	% carried out by overseas offices
Mitsubishi	536 069	6.1	20.6
Mitsui	660 599	7.9	42.2
C. Itoh	784 140	11.9	20.4
Marubeni	836 367	13.3	2.5
Sumitomo	304 445	5.2	11.1
Nissho Iwai	411 960	9.9	21.5
Tomen	351 522	16.5	17.2
Kanematsu Gosho	164 787	8.1	1.0
Nichimen Jitsugyo	270 061	15.1	27.2

Source: Adapted from Kyoikusha, Sogo Shosha no Keiei Hikaku (Comparison of
General Trading Companies' Management) Kyoikusha, Tokyo 1980, pp. 248-250.

Table 5a

TRADING COMPANIES'OVERSEAS MANUFACTURING VENTURES (1980)

By Industry	Number of Ventures	% of Ventures
Textiles	152	22.3
Metals* & metal products**	134	19.6
Chemicals	118	17.3
Food processing	63	9.2
Electric machinery	47	6.9
Non-electric machinery	27	3.9
Transport equipment	26	3.8
Iron and steel	15	2.2
Stone, clay and glass	12	1.8
Sundries	88	12.9
Total	682	100.0

*   Non-ferrous metals only

**   Both ferrous and non-ferrous. Among these metal products, galvanised iron
        plate accounted for 30 ventures or 4.4%

Table 5b

TOP-NINE TRADING COMPANIES' MANUFACTURING VENTURES
(by type*, 1980)

	A	A'	B	B'	C	C'	D	D'
Textiles		3	12	1	22	5	109	
Metals & metal products	1	1	11	2	21	7	55	6
Chemicals			6	4	14	4	88	2
Food processing	4	1	3	2	27	2	23	3
Electrical machinery			2	1	4		34	6
Non-electrical machinery			5				22	
Transport equipment			2		5		18	1
Iron & steel							15	
Stone, clay and glass			2		1		9	
Sundries		1	13	4	12	3	52	3
Total ventures (682) By type	5	6	56	12	108	21	452	22
Percentage	0.7	0.9	8.2	1.8	15.8	3.1	66.3	3.2

Type A (or A'): Ventures wholly-owned by the home (or a regional) office of a trading company

Type B (or B'): Joint ventures owned by the home (or a regional) office of a trading company and a Japanese company or companies. They are wholly-owned by Japanese interests.

Type C (or C'): Joint ventures between the home (or a regional) office of a trading company and local interests.

Type D (or D'): Joint ventures among the home (or a regional) office of a trading company, a Japanese company or companies, and local interests (and/or third-country interests).

Table 5c

TRADING COMPANIES' OWNERSHIP INTEREST IN OVERSEAS MANUFACTURING VENTURES, 1980

Equity Participation	Mitsui	Mitsubishi	Marubeni	C. Itoh	Sumitomo	Nissho Iwai	Kanematsu	Tomen	Nichimen	Total ventures by ownership No.	%
1 - 9%	40	27	20	22	23	20	10	11	11	184	26.9
10 - 29%	62	44	50	47	25	28	22	24	25	327	47.9
30 - 49%	21	16	17	22	3	8	7	1	5	100	14.7
50%	0	6	6	1	1	0	0	1	1	16	2.3
51 - 79%	3	2	2	3	1	2	1	3	2	19	2.8
80 - 100%	5	1	5	4	3	0	3	4	1	26	3.8
	(2)*	(0)	(3)	(3)	(0)		(1)	(1)	(1)	(11)	
n.a.	0	2	3	0	4	1	0	0	0	10	1.5
Total ventures by company	131	98	103	99	60	59	43	44	45	682	100.0

* The figures in parentheses show number of 100% ownership included in the 80 - 100% category

n.a.: not available

Table 5d

TRADING COMPANIES' JOINT OWNERSHIP WITH OTHER JAPANESE INVESTORS IN OVERSEAS MANUFACTURING VENTURES (1980)

Equity Participation	Mitsui	Mitsubishi	Marubeni	C. Itoh	Sumitomo	Nissho Iwai	Kanematsu	Tomen	Nichimen	Total ventures No.	Total ventures %
1 - 29%	32	25	23	25	21	19	13	9	10	177	25.9
30 - 49%	34	27	29	33	10	15	5	11	16	180	26.4
50%	20	17	13	3	4	3	2	4	6	72	10.6
51 - 79%	19	6	17	13	9	9	9	7	5	94	13.8
80 - 100%	26	22	18	25	13	12	14	13	8	151	22.1
	(11)*	(12)	(14)	(14)	(17)	(6)	(8)	(5)	(3)	(90)	13.2
n.a.	0	1	3	0	3	1	0	0	0	8	1.2
Total	131	98	103	99	60	59	43	44	45	682	100.0

*   The figures in parentheses show number of 100% ownership included in the 80 - 100% category

n.a.: not available

Table 5e

LOCATION OF TRADING COMPANIES' OVERSEAS MANUFACTURING VENTURES, 1980

Regions	Mitsui	Mitsubishi	Marubeni	C. Itoh	Sumitomo	Nissho Iwai	Kanematsu	Tomen	Nichimen	Total by region No.	Total by region %
Developing regions										547	80.2
Asia:											
Rep. of Korea	11	9	4	5	4	2	2	4	3	44	
Taiwan	7	9	3	8	1	0	4	1	0	33	
Hong Kong	0	3	1	3	0	1	2	1	1	12	
Singapore	8	1	5	4	6	6	2	1	1	34	
Thailand	16	14	9	5	4	3	2	7	3	64	
Indonesia	16	6	8	10	7	7	3	7	8	71	
Philippines	3	7	6	4	0	4	5	6	2	37	
Malaysia	9	5	6	6	4	1	2	4	6	43	
Others	5	1	2	4	1	1	2	3	7	26	
Sub-total	75	55	44	49	27	25	24	34	31	364	53.4
Latin America:											
Brazil	7	7	134	17	10	11	7	7	2	81	
Mexico	2	3	3	1	1	0	0	0	1	11	
Venezuela	1	1	3	0	1	2	2	0	0	10	
Others	11	3	5	7	1	1	1	0	3	32	
Sub-total	21	14	24	25	13	14	10	7	6	134	19.6
Africa:	4	5	6	4	1	5	2	0	5	32	4.7
Middle East	2	2	4	3	1	3	0	1	1	17	2.5
Developed regions										135	19.8
North America	14	11	18	8	12	5	5	2	2	77	11.2
Europe	12	5	2	5	1	2	1	0	0	28	4.1
Oceania	3	6	5	5	5	5	1	0	0	30	4.4
Total by company	131	98	103	99	60	59	43	44	45	682	100.0

Table 5f

MAJOR DIRECT LOANS TO MANUFACTURING AFFILIATES OVERSEAS (LOANS FROM JAPAN ONLY)

Trader	Debtor (line of business)	Trader's Equity Interest %	Millions of Yen	Amount of Loan (in millions of Yen)	Maturity
Mitsui & Co.	P.T. Somen Nusantra, Indonesia (cement)	35	2 162	6 253	1986
	P.T. Gaya Persaki Synthetic (textiles)	65	1 381	2 761	1985
	Soryu Cement, South Korea (cement)	No equity interest		15 155 000 $US (with Marubeni Corp.)	1984 (11 years)
Mitsubishi Corporation	Mitsubishi Kramayudha Motors Mf., Indonesia (auto parts)	25	494	1 769	1986
	Eastern Polymer, Indonesia (chemicals)	30	248	480	1986
	Petrokimika Kayaku, Indonesia	20	60	188	1985
	Malaysia Vegetable Oil Refinery, Malaysia vegetable oil	25	267	197	1983
	ATR Wire & Cable, USA (metal products)	20		407	1988
	MCF Footwear Corp., USA (footwear)	51 (by Mitsubishi International, USA)	4 747	3 169	1989
	Carib Isoprene Corp., Porto Rico (chemicals)	40	942	1 174	1982
	Eidai de Brasil Madeiras S.A. Brazil (plywood)	94	1 390	177	1983
	Namascor N.V., Holland (metal products)	49	784	221	1985
	Tekkosha Hellas ABE, Greece (chemicals)	35	886	380	1987
Marubeni Corporation	Budidharma Jakarta, Indonesia (metal products)	27	1 048	2 454	1984
	Kuraray Manunggal Fiber, Indonesia (textiles)	30	87	2 096	1986
	Pranburi Sugar Industry, Thailand (food)	28	1 200	1 956	1997
C. Itoh & Co.	Penging Tex Sdn Bhd., Malaysia (textiles)	49	390	988	1979
	Jakarta Kyoei Steel, Indonesia (metal products)	37	267	1 030	1985
	Thai Teijin Textiles, Thailand (textiles)	24	215	812	1984
	Electro Alloys Corp., Philippines	20	4 300	1 620	1987
	Karibe S.A. Industria e Comercio, Brazil (textiles)	35	238	1 503	1982
Sumitomo Corporation	P.T. Central Java Marine Products, Indonesia (food)	80	235	122	1985
	Nigerian Wire & Cable (electric products)	20	94	453	1986
Nissho Iwai	P.T. Serniwa Steel Works, Indonesia (metal products)	35	468	626	1987
	P.T. Kanebo-Nissho Iwai Sahabat, Indonesia (textiles)	35	159	1 730	1988
	Asian Transmission Corp., Philippines	30	166	263	1986
	Kobe Alumina Associates, Australia (metals)	35	198	984	1998
Kanematsu Gosho Tomen	Fil-Mosaic Corp., Philippines (ceramics)	12		48	1982
	P.T. Teijin, Indonesia Fiber Corp., Indonesia (textiles)	20	1 470	1 361	1985
	Eastern Chemical Co., Thailand (chemicals)	27	134	719	1986
	Korea Polyol, South Korea (chemicals)	45	310	161	1985
Nichimen Jitsugyo	P.T. Tobu Indonesia Steel Co., Indonesia (metal products)	75	300	1 983	1989
	P.T. Kalimantan Steel, Indonesia (metal products)	50	144	212	1986
	P.T. Musahi, Indonesia (metal products)	35	23	43	1986
	P.T. Baninusa, Indonesia (metal products)	23	91	621	1986
	P.T. Mitra Kartica Sejati, Indonesia (food)	30	35	74	1984

Source: Compiled from Keizai Chosa Kyokai, Kigyobetsu Kaigai Toshi. Jojo Kigyo hen (Overseas Investments by Enterprises. The Enterprises listed on the Exchange Market), Keizai Chosa Kyokai, Tokyo, 1982.

Table 6a

JAPAN'S DEPENDENCE ON IMPORTED RESOURCES AND ITS SHARE OF WORLD IMPORTS
(COMPARISON WITH U.S. AND WEST GERMANY)

Commodity	Import Dependency Ratio				Share of World Imports			
	Japan		U.S. / W. Germany 1980		Japan		U.S. / W. Germany 1980	
	1963 %	1980 %	U.S. %	W. Germany %	1962 %	1980 %	U.S. %	W. Germany %
Iron ore	76.7	98.7	28.3	96.3	26.1	41.1	10.9	16.6
Copper ore	59.6	96.0	37.4	99.8	7.0	23.4	11.3	13.4
Lead	51.1	83.9	48.6	90.6	4.4	6.6	5.8	13.4
Zinc	32.6	68.5	54.5	70.2	3.7	9.0	18.2	12.9
Bauxite	100.0	100.0	65.1	100.0	3.3	20.0	15.9	14.8
Nickel	100.0	100.0	90.2	100.0	4.2	5.6	37.9	13.9
Coal	46.9	81.8	-9.6*	--8.7	8.4	26.3	0.7	3.8
Petroleum	98.8	99.8	42.3	95.8	7.3	14.1	18.8	6.4
Natural gas	0	90.7	5.8	65.8	0	10.4	19.2	20.5
Timber	24.6	68.3	2.2	22.5	13.4	21.9	17.8	6.7
Wool	100.0	100.0	26.4	91.1	18.3	15.3	2.2	6.9
Cotton	100.0	100.0	302.3*	100.0	17.2	14.3	0.1	3.8
Soybean	n.a.	95.8	-78.7*	100.0	n.a.	16.0	0	14.2
Corn	n.a.	100.0	-59.7*	76.7	11.8	16.0	0	2.9
Wheat	n.a.	90.5	-133.4*	--5.9	7.0	5.8	0	1.3

* Indicates degree to which country depends on export markets.

Sources: 1963 figures for Japan from Keizai Shingikai (Economic Deliberation Council), Kokusaika jidai no Shigen Mondai (Resource Issues in the Era of Internationalization), Tokyo 1970, p. 12, 1963, figures from Jukagaku Kogyo, Nihon no Kaigai Shigen Kaihatsu (Japan's Overseas Resource Development), Tokyo, 1976, p. 36 and 1980 statistics from Japan's Ministry of International Trade and Industry, Tsusho Hakusho (White Paper on International Trade), Tokyo, 1982, pp. 404-405.

Table 6b

SUPPLY OF IMPORTED IRON ORE TO MAJOR STEEL MAKERS, BY COMPANY, 1978
(in 10 000 tons)

Trading Company	Japan Steel	Nippon Kokan	Kawasaki Steel	Sumitomo Metal	Kobe Steel	Nisshin Steel	Total by Trading Company Volume	%
Mitsubishi	714	455	277	293	152	82	1 973	19.0
Mitsui	1 432	183	227	209	129	78	2 258	21.8
C. Itoh	484	79	287	116	57	20	1 043	10.1
Marubeni	516	652	117	267	170	30	1 752	16.9
Sumitomo	70	17	27	682	7	4	807	7.8
Nissho Iwai	796	98	133	84	427	75	1 613	15.6
Tomen	95	163	116	62	26	13	475	4.6
Kanematsu Gosho	42	5	13	9	22	3	94	0.9
Nichimen Jitsugyo	142	92	41	32	11	20	338	3.3
							10 353	100.0

Source: Adapted from Kyoikusha, Sogo Shosha no Keiei Hikaku (Comparison of General Trading Companies' Management), Kyoikusha, Tokyo, 1980, p. 97.

Table 6c

SUPPLY OF IMPORTED COKING COAL TO MAJOR STEEL MAKERS BY TOP NINE TRADING COMPANIES, 1978
(in 10 000 tons)

Trading Company	Japan Steel	Nippon Kokan	Kawasaki Steel	Sumitomo Metal	Kobe Steel	Nisshin Steel	Total by Trading Company Volume	%
Mitsubishi	623	291	284	287	129	73	1 687	34.4
Mitsui	703	156	152	175	134	26	1 346	27.4
C. Itoh	157	53	100	56	18	1	385	7.8
Marubeni	110	160	45	29	29	14	387	7.9
Sumitomo	85	39	7	219	13	2	365	7.4
Nissho Iwai	114	4	4	5	56	18	201	4.1
Tomen	93	69	27	31	18	5	243	4.9
Kanematsu Gosho	22	0	0	0	0	0	22	0.4
Nichimen Jitsugyo	132	85	27	2	21	3	270	5.5
							4 906	100.0

Source: Adapted from Kyoikusha, Sogo Shosha no Keiei Hikaku (Comparison of General Trading Companies' Management), Kyoikusha, Tokyo, 1980, p. 97.

Table 7a

RESOURCE DEVELOPMENT VENTURES BY SECTOR OF TOP NINE TRADING COMPANIES, 1980

	Mitsui	Mitsubishi	Marubeni	C. Itoh	Sumitomo	Nissho Iwai	Tomen	Kanematsu	Nichimen	Total Ventures Number	Total Ventures %
Iron ore	2	3	3	4	3	2	2	1	1	21	15.1
Non-ferrous metals	7	3	6	3	10	3	0	0	0	32	23.0
Coal	4	4	2	0	3	0	0	0	0	13	9.4
Oil and natural gas	1	2	2	0	0	1	0	0	0	6	4.3
Combination of above	0	0	2	1	0	0	0	0	0	3	2.0
Agriculture & animal husbandry	4	6	4	6	1	0	2	0	1	24	17.3
Fishery and processing	4	5	3	6	0	1	21	0	1	22	15.8
Forestry and lumbering	5	6	1	3	0	1	0	2	0	18	12.9
Total by company	27	29	23	23	17	8	6	3	3	139	100.0

Table 7b

MAJOR TRADING COMPANIES' CAPITAL PARTICIPATION IN URANIUM DEVELOPMENT CORPORATIONS

Corporation	Activity	Trading company
1. Australia Uranium Mine Exploration Corp.	Exploration works in Australia, joint venture with AGIP Nuclear Australia Co. (Italy)	C. Itoh (61%) Sumitomo Metal & Mining (20%) Furukawa Kogyo (10%) Mitsubishi Metal (9%)
2. Uranium Development Corporation	Exploration works in Australia, joint venture with Denison Co. (Canada)	Mitsui & Co. (70%) Mitsui Metal & Smelting (30%)
3. Taihei Uranium Mine Exploration Corp.	Exploration works in the U.S., joint venture with Mineral Recovery Co. (U.S.)	Mitsubishi Corporation (40%) Mitsubishi Metal (60%)
4. Tokyo Uranium Development Corporation	Exploration works in Mauritania, joint venture with French interests	Marubeni Corporation (57%) Nippon Mining (39%) Fuji Bank (5%) Nippon Kogyo Bank (5%) Yasuda Marine Fire Insurance (2.5%)
5. Mississippi Uranium Corporation	Exploration works in the U.S. in a joint venture with Texas Gulf (U.S.)	Nissho Iwai (50%) Dowa Kogyo (50%)
6. Kyodo Uranium Development Corporation	Exploration works in the U.S. in a joint venture with PUK (France)	Sumitomo Corporation (30%) Mitsubishi Corporation (20%) Sumitomo Metal & Mining (10%) Mitsubishi Metal (20%) Mitsubishi Mining & Cement (20%)

Table 7c

1.	Mitsui Petroleum Development Corporation	Mitsui & Co. and other 40 Mitsui group companies, including petroleum and mining companies and banks
2.	Mitsubishi Petroleum Development Corporation	Mitsubishi Corporation and other 29 Mitsubishi group companies
3.	Fuyo Petroleum Development Corporation	Marubeni Corporation, Fuji Bank, Nippon Kokan, and other 36 Fuyo group companies
4.	Sumitomo Petroleum Development Corporation	Sumitomo Corporation and other 42 Sumitomo group companies
5.	World Energy Development Corporation	C. Itoh & Co., Kanematsu Gosho, Kawasaki Steel, Daiichi Kangyo Bank, and other 44 Daiichi Kangyo group companies
6.	Toyo Petroleum Development	Nissho Iwai, Nichimen, Sanwa Bank, Maruzen Oil, and other 33 Sanwa group companies
7.	Central Energy Development Corporation	Tomen, Toyo Oil, Tokai Bank, Daikyo Oil, and other 41 Tokai group companies

Table 7a

RESOURCE DEVELOPMENT LOANS EXTENDED FROM JAPAN BY TRADING COMPANIES

(By regional distribution and trading companies' equity interest in debtor companies at the end of January 1982)

	Mitsui	Mitsubishi	Marubeni	C. Itoh	Sumitomo	Nissho Iwai	Tomen	Kanematsu	Nichimen	Total loans Number	%
Developing region											
Asia	3	5	1	1	1	2	1		2	16	34.8
Latin America	1	3	1	1	2	2				10	21.7
Africa	1									1	2.2
Middle East									1	1	2.2
Developed region											
North America	1	5		2	2					10	21.7
Oceania	3	3		1		1				8	17.4
Total by company	9	16	2	5	5	5	1	0	3	46	100.0
% by company	19.6	34.8	4.3	10.9	10.9	10.9	2.2		6.5		
Equity interest											
None	3	8	2	4	4	4				25	54.3
Below 49%	3	2			1	1	1			8	
50% - 79%	1	3		1						5	45.7
80% - 100%	2	3							3	8	
Total	9	16	2	5	5	5	1	0	3	46	100.0

Table 7e

RESOURCE DEVELOPMENT LOANS EXTENDED BY TRADING COMPANIES FROM JAPAN
(By sectorial distribution and by value at end of January 1982)

	Mitsui	Mitsubishi	Marubeni	C. Itoh	Sumitomo	Nissho Iwai	Tomen	Kanematsu	Nichimen	Total Ventures Number	%
Sector											
Agribusiness	1	1								2	4.3
Fishery	2	1							1	4	8.7
Forestry	2	3	1	1						7	15.2
Oil & gas	2		1				1			4	8.7
Iron ore	2	2		1	2	1				8	17.4
Copper ore		7		2	3	3			2	17	37.0
Other non-ferrous		1		1		1				3	6.5
Coal		1								1	2.2
Total by company	9	16	2	5	5	5	1	0	3	46	100.0
Value											
Less than Yen 1 billion	2	11	1	1	1	1	1		3	21	45.7
Above Yen 1 billion but below Yen 5 billion	3	2	1	3	1	2				12	26.1
Above Yen 5 billion but below Yen 10 billion				1	1					2	4.3
Above Yen 10 billion	3	1								4	8.7
n.a.	1	2			2	2				7	15.2
Total by company	9	16	2	5	5	5	1	0	3	46	100.0

Table 8

PLANT EXPORTS BY TOP NINE TRADING COMPANIES AND THEIR MAJOR PARTNERS,
APRIL 1979 - MARCH 1980

Trading Company	Major export partners	Value of plant exports (Yen 100 mn.)
Mitsui	Toshiba, TEC, Mitsui Shipbuilding	4 000
Mitsubishi	Mitsubishi Heavy Industries Mitsubishi Electric	5 000
C. Itoh	Nippon Steel, Kobe Steel	3 300
Marubeni	Hitachi Kawasaki Heavy Industries, Niigata Engineering	6 000
Sumitomo	Sumitomo Denko, Sumitomo Heavy Industries, Nippon Electric Meidensha, Toshiba	2 000
Nissho Iwai	Hitachi Shipbuilding, Kobe Steel	3 600
Tomen	Meidensha, Toyoda Automatic Loom, Teijin	500
Kanematsu Gosho	Fuji Electric, Hitachi	600
Nichimen Jitsugyo	Ishikawajima-Harima Industries Niigata Engineering	1 200

Source: Jukagaku Kogyo Tsushin, 1981 -- Plant Yushutsu no Genjo to Tenbou
(1981 -- Present Status and Future Prospects for Plant Exports), Tokyo,
1980, p. 1.

NOTES AND REFERENCES

1. New forms of investment are defined and discussed in Charles Oman, New Forms of International Investment in Developing Countries, OECD Development Centre, 1984.

2. Kozo Yamamura, "General Trading Companies in Japan: Their Origins and Growth", in Hugh Patrick, ed., Japanese Industrialization and its Social Consequences, University of California Press, Berkeley, Calif., 1976, p. 169. For an analysis of Mitsui's history, see also John G. Roberts, Mitsui: Three Centuries of Japanese Business, Weatherhill, New York, 1973.

3. K. Kato and K. Noda (ed.), Sumitomo Shoji, Sohyohsha, Tokyo, 1980.

4. This choice is mentioned in G. C. Allen, Japan's Economic Expansion, Oxford University Press, London, 1965, p. 173.

5. For an excellent analysis of the sale of state enterprises, see Thomas C. Smith, Political Change and Industrial Development in Japan: Government Enterprise, 1868-1880, Stanford University Press, Palo Alto, 1955.

6. This section draws on Terutomo Ozawa, "Japan's Industrial Groups", MSU-Business Topics, Vol. 28, N°4, Autumn 1980, pp. 33-41.

7. Yamamura, op. cit., p. 167.

8. Ibid., p. 179.

9. This source of income is derogatorily called "a slumber commission" or nemuri kohsen in Japan.

10. Ibid., pp. 36-39.

11. K. Kato and K. Noda (ed.), Mitsui Bussan, Sohyohsha, Tokyo, 1980, pp. 38-40.

12. Yutaka Matsumoto, "Shosha no Hachijunendai Senryaku" (Strategies of General Trading Companies for the 1980s), Chuo Koron, N°74, Spring 1980, p. 149.

13. Hitoshi Misonou, "Sogo Sosha wa Shayo de aruka?" (Is the Sogo Sosha Declining?), Ekonomisto, Tokyo, May 1961.

14. Peter F. Drucker, "Economic Realities and Enterprise Strategy", in Ezra F. Vogel, ed., Modern Japanese Organization and Decision-Making, University of California Press, Berkeley, Calif., 1975, pp. 238-239.

15. The equivalent of $59.6 million at the exchange rate of $1 = Yen 200

16. Kyosuke Arita, Sogo Shosha: Mirai no Kozu o Saguru, (General Trading Companies: An Examination of Their Future Plans), Nihon Keizai Shimbunsha, Tokyo, 1976, p. 97.

17. Ibid., p 98.

18. The experiences of Mitsubishi Corporation are documented in Kato and Noda (ed.), Mitsubishi Shoji, op. cit., pp. 23-25.

19. Ministry of International Trade and Industry, Hachijunendai no Sangyo Kozo no Tenbo to Kadai, (Prospects for, and Problems of, Industrial Structure during the 1980s), Tokyo, 1981, p. 292.

20. "The Social Organization of Decision Making in the Multinational Corporation", in David E. Apter and Louis Wolf Goodman, eds., The Multinational Corporation and Social Change, Praeger, New York, 1976, pp. 64-65.

21. Mitsubishi's overseas trading ventures are the most "independent" as far as third-country trade is concerned (42 per cent share), whereas Marubeni, the most active in third-country trade, is adopting a centralised operation, since only 2.5 per cent can be credited "purely" to its overseas ventures. In the same vein, Kanematsui's third-country trade is highly centralised in the home office.

22. At the time of writing, Iran was imposing a unique counter-purchase system on Japan's big trading companies, which have long-term crude oil import contracts with the Iranian Government. It allows the traders to export products up to only half the value of their crude imports. Thus Iran's counter-purchase requirement is in effect as high as 200 per cent.

23. This conceptual distinction is made in Kiyoshi Kojima, Development Oriented Direct Foreign Investment and the Role of ADB, Report N°4, Asian Development Bank, April 1982.

24. The most active investor in this product is Mitsui & Co. It operates, among others, the following ventures.

   -- Elizabeth Steel Consolidated, in the Philippines, is a joint venture set up by Mitsui & Co. (1.2 per cent interest), Japan Steel (0.6 per cent interest), and local interests (98.2 per cent). It is capitalised at 23.3 million pesos and employs 800 workers.

   -- Thailand Iron Works, Thailand, is a joint venture set up by Mitsui & Co. (36.2 per cent interest), Azuma Steel (3.8 per cent interest), and local interests (60 per cent). It is capitalised at 15 million bahts and employs 276 workers.

   -- P. T. Fumira, Indonesia, is a joint venture set up by Mitsui (30 per cent interest), Japan Steel (30 per cent interest), and local interests (40 per cent). It is capitalised at 81.5 billion rupiahs and employs 225 workers.

25. Other examples: Bangkok Weaving Mills, Thailand, is a joint venture set up by Mitsubishi Corporation (25 per cent interest), Toyo Textiles (0.4 per cent interest), and local interest, (74.6 per cent). It produces cotton yarns and fabrics and employs 2 000 workers. Kolon Polyester Inc., South Korea, was set up by Toray (19.8 per cent interest), Mitsui & Co. (8.2 per cent interest), and local interests (72 per cent). It produces polyester filaments and yarns and has 1 950 workers. Thai Teijin Textiles, Thailand, a joint venture established by Teijin (25 per cent interest), C. Itoh (24 per cent interest) and local interests (51 per cent). It produces polyester-rayon yarns and fabrics. There are 1 919 employees. Over 1 000 workers are employed by P. T. Unitex, Indonesia, a joint venture set up by Unichika (35 per cent interest), Marubeni Corporation (20 per cent interest), and local interests (45 per cent). It produces polyester-cotton blends.

26. Of the 682 overseas manufacturing ventures, 15 (2.2 per cent) were set up between 1950 and 1959, 142 (20.8 per cent) between 1960-1969, 343 (50.3 per cent between 1970-1975 and 147 (26.6 per cent) between 1976 and 1980. Figures were not available for 35 ventures.

27. The four joint ventures are: Textile Alliance Ltd. (TAL) is a synthetic fabric manufacturing company owned by Toray Industries (49.9 per cent interest), C. Itoh (9.2 per cent interest), and local interests (48.9 per cent); Textile Amalgamated Ltd. is in charge of marketing TAL's products both locally and abroad. It is owned by Toray Industries (20 per cent interest), C. Itoh (20 per cent interest), TAL (26.7 per cent interest), and local interests (33.3 per cent); C.T.T. International Ltd. is engaged in the procurement of raw materials for TAL. It is owned by Toray Industries (21.43 per cent interest), C. Itoh (7.14 per cent interest), and local interests (71.43 per cent); Lissenden Investments Ltd. is a holding company set up by Toray Industries (45 per cent interest), C. Itoh (4 per cent interest), and local interests (51 per cent). In addition, TAL itself has two other subsidiaries which are owned jointly on a 50-50 basis with Toray Industries: one is involved in fabric dyeing, and the other in knitting.

28. The first is Canlubang Automotive Resources, a D-type assembly venture set up by Mitsubishi Motor (17.5 per cent interest), Nissho-Iwai (17.5 per cent interest), and local interests (65 per cent). It employs 1 421 workers. The second is Asian Transmission Co., a D-type venture which produces transmissions for the Canlubang Automotive Resources. It is owned by Mitsubishi Motor (30 per cent interest), Nissho-Iwai (30 per cent interest), Canlubang Automobile Resources (30 per cent interest), and local interests (10 per cent). It employs 394 workers. The third is Apex Motor Manufacturing Corporation, a D-type venture engaged in the production of a variety of car parts and components and owned by Kayaba Kogyo (22.22 per cent interest), Nissho-Iwai (3.7 per cent), and local interests (74.08 per cent). It employs 30 workers. The fourth is FMI Manufacturing Corporation, a C-type trading venture (despite its misleading name) engaged in the import and sales of car parts and owned by Nissho-Iwai (30 per cent interest) and local interests (70 per cent).

29. Yoshihide Uchida, _Shosha_ (Tokyo: Kyoikusha, 1982), p.152. See also

Table 2 for an estimate of the equity-debt ratio of overseas investment for each of the nine companies.

30. Estimated from the data published in Toyo Keizai, Kaigai Shinshutsu Kigyo Soran (Japanese Multinationals Facts & Figures), Toyo Keizai, Tokyo, 1981.

31. The operations of these governmental organisations are described in Terutomo Ozawa, Multinationalism, Japanese Style: the Political Economy of Outward Dependency, Princeton University Press, Princeton, N.J. 1979.

32. Japan's Ministry of International Trade and Industry, Wagakuni Kigyo no Kaigaijigyo Katsudo [Overseas Business Activities of Japanese Enterprises]. N°.9 report, 1980, p.15.

33. Computed from data in Kyoikusha, Sogo Shosha no Keiei Hikaku (Comparison of General Trading Companies' Management), Kyoikusha, Tokyo, 1980, p.101.

34. These are types D and D', which include a trading company, another Japanese company and local and/or third country interests.

35. This tendency is even more pronounced in the smaller trading companies. None of the overseas regional offices of Nissho-Iwai, Tomen, and Nichimen, for example, is involved as an investor in resource development (that is, there is no incidence of A', B', C' or D' type ventures).

36. $1 = 250 yen.

37. Based in part on information in Kokusai Keizai (International Economy), a special report on ASEAN, Vol. 16, No. 8, July 31, 1979, p.212.

38. Ministry of International Trade and Industry, Japanese Government, 1980-Tsusho Hakusho (White Paper on International Trade), 1980, p.247

39. Some specific examples of resource-development loans are:

    -- A joint long-term loan of US $2 376 000 was offered by Mitsui, Mitsubishi, Sumitomo, and Nissho-Iwai in 1973 to a copper mining company in Peru in exchange for a long-term purchase contract for crude copper.

    -- A 12-and-half-year loan of US $50 million was given by C. Itoh, Marubeni, Sumitomo, Mitsubishi, and Mitsui to Minercoes Brasil Reunidas, Brazil, to develop an iron ore mine.

    -- A loan of 3 150 million Yen was extended by C. Itoh to the Batong Buhai Co. of the Philippines to develop a new copper mine and to supply 3 000 tons of copper ore annually.

    -- A loan of 2 783 million Yen (with maturity in 1996) was given by Mitsubishi Corporation to the P.T. Balikpapan Forest Industries of

Indonesia, a joint venture in which Mitsubishi has 80 per cent equity interest (in the amount of 1 586 million Yen).

40. In 1966, Japan exported 90 plants at a value of $327 million. By 1979, exports had shot up to 743 plants, valued at $11 785 million.

41. Examples of these ventures are:

-- International Marine Construction, SAK, Kuwait, is a joint venture between Japanese interests (49 per cent), consisting of Nippon Steel (12 per cent), Mitsui (8 per cent), Marubeni (8 per cent), Nissho-Iwai (8 per cent), C. Itoh (7 per cent) and Mitsubishi (6 per cent) and local interests (51 per cent). The venture specialises in off-shore installations and engineering for petroleum and natural gas wells.

-- Pacific Consultant do Brasil, Engenharia Civil Arquitetura Ltds, Brazil, is a joint venture between Japanese interests (79.76 per cent) represented by eight trading companies (Mitsui, Mitsubishi, C. Itoh, Marubeni, Sumitomo, Nissho-Iwai, Tomen, and Nichimen) and local interests. It was established in 1972 and is engaged in construction consulting.

-- P. T. Promits Engineering & Construction, Indonesia, is a joint venture set up by Mitsui & Co. (55 per cent interest), Koyo Construction Co. (10 per cent), Toray Engineering (5 per cent), Taihen Dengyo (10 percent), and local interests (20 per cent). It is capitalised at $1 million and employs 245 people. The venture, set up in 1973, specialises in plant installation, civil engineering and engineering designing.

-- Hyosam Control Maintenance Co., South Korea, is a joint venture set up in 1979 by Mitsubishi Electric (25.5 per cent), Mitsubishi Corporation (8.5 per cent) and local interests (66 per cent). The venture is engaged in providing maintenance and repair work for electric machinery used in steel mills.

42. These ventures can be broken down into five A and A' types, three B and B' types, seven C and C' types, and eight D and D' types. To cite some examples:

-- Southern Cross Carriers, Singapore, is a joint venture between Japanese interests, Mitsui & Co. (49 per cent interest), and Utoku Transport (26 per cent) and local interests (25 per cent). It specialises in warehousing and trans-shipping of chemicals.

-- Armazens Gerais Tozan S.A., Brazil, is a warehousing venture jointly owned by Japanese interests, Mitsubishi Corporation (16.67 per cent interest) and Mitsubishi

-- Warehousing (55.55 per cent) and local interests (27.78 per cent).

-- New Port Bulk Terminal, Malaysia, is a wholly-owned port terminal of Sumitomo Corporation. It handles liquid chemicals.

43. Some examples are: P. T. Moges Shipping Company, Indonesia, which is a joint venture of Mitsui & Co. (13 per cent interest), Mitsui O.S.K. (26 per cent), and Lloyds (61 per cent); Coldgad Trading, Bermuda, is a transport company for liquified natural gas, set up by Mitsubishi Corporation (50 per cent), and Shell group (50 per cent); Trinity Maritime Corporation, Liberia, is a tripartite joint venture among C. Itoh (20 per cent) Iino Shipping (40 per cent) and local interests (40 per cent).

44. Some examples are:

-- Pan Malaysia Cement Works, Malaysia, is a local holding company participated in by Marubeni Corporation (2 per cent interest). It is a holding company of cement producers.

-- Hong Kong United Industries, Hong Kong, is a local investment company owned by Japanese interests (Mitsubishi Corporation, 9.1 per cent, and Tokuyama Soda, 9.5 per cent), and local banks.

-- Venturetek International, Canada, is an investment company that specialises in investing in local venture businesses. Participants are, Daiichi Kangyo Bank, Mitsubishi Bank, and Mitsubishi Corporation, which together hold 3.3 per cent interest.

-- Sumitomo Australia Development, Australia, is an investment company wholly-owned by the Sumitomo group. Sumitomo Corporation, the largest shareholder, owns 26.5 per cent interest; Sumitomo Metal 16 per cent; Sumitomo Bank 10 per cent; Sumitomo Electric, Sumitomo Trust Bank, and other members of the group hold the balance. This Sumitomo group venture develops and invests in large-scale resource extraction projects.

45. Mitsui owns the Boonmitr Building Co. in Bangkok, Thailand, and Trade & Industrial Development in Singapore. Sumitomo has the Sumisho Development Co. in Bangkok, while Marubeni set up the Marubeni Benelux Development S.A. in Brussels, the Deutsch-Japanisches Center GmbH in Dusseldorf, and the Marubeni Brasil Representacoes & Participacoes Ltda in Sao Paulo.

46. To cite some examples:

-- Hotel Shilla Co., South Korea, is a joint venture between Korean interests (80 per cent) and a group of Japanese companies that includes Nissho-Iwai, Taisei Construction, Taisei Kanko, among others. It constructed the Hotel Shilla and now manages it.

-- Mauna Loa Land in Hawaii, was set up by Tokyu Corporation (42.4 per cent interest), Mitsubishi Corporation (11.4 per cent), and other Japanese interests to develop a comprehensive resort consisting of a hotel, a golf course, condominiums and other facilities.

47. At the conceptual level, the benefits of trade can be considered as consisting of two components: a gain from specialisation in production (i.e. a resource-reallocative gain) and a gain from exchange itself (i.e. a transactional gain). In the absence of an effective inter-

national marketing (or procurement) capacity on the part of developing countries, not only is the transactional gain often captured entirely by foreign buyers (or sellers) but part, if not all, of the gain from specialisation itself may also be lost.

48. J. Panglaykim, Indonesia's Economic and Business Relations with ASEAN and Japan. Centre for Strategic and International Studies, Jakarta, 1977, pp.162-164.

49. D. H. Robertson, Control of Industry, Nisbet, London, 1930, p.85.

50. R. H. Coase, "The Nature of the Firm", Economica, N.S., Vol. IV, Nos.13-16, 1937, pp.386-405.

51. Stephen Hymer, "The Efficiency (Contradictions) of Multinational Corporations," American Economic Review, Vol. LX, No.2, May 1970, pp.441-453.

52. S. H. Hymer, "The International Operations of National Firms: A Study of Direct Foreign Investment", Ph.D. dissertation, M.I.T., 1960 (published by M.I.T. Press, 1976). C. P. Kindleberger, American Business Abroad: Six Lectures on Direct Investment, Yale University Press, New Haven, Conn., 1969). R. E. Caves, "International Corporations: The Industrial Economics of Foreign Investment", Economica, 38, February 1971, pp.1-27. R. Vernon, "International Investment and International Trade in the Product Cycle", Quarterly Journal of Economics, 80, May 1966, pp.190-207. R. Z. Aliber, "A Theory of Direct Foreign Investment", in C. P. Kindleberger (ed.), The International Corporation: A Symposium, Chapter 1 M.I.T. Press, Cambridge, Mass., 1970. S. P. Magee, "Information and Multinational Corporations: An Appropriability Theory of Direct Foreign Investent", in J. Bhagwati (ed.), The New International Economic Order M.I.T. Press, Cambridge, Mass., 1977, pp.317-40. H. G. Grubel, "International Diversified Portfolios: Welfare Gains and Capital Flows", American Economic Review, 58, December 1968, pp.1299-314. A. M. Rugman, International Diversification and the Multinational Enterprise, Lexington Books, Lexington, Md., 1979. T. Agmon and D. Lessard, "Investor Recognition of Corporate International Diversification", Journal of Finance, 32, September 1977, pp.1049-55.

53. P. J. Buckley and M. C. Casson, The Future of the Multinational Enterprise, London: Macmillan, 1976, and M. C. Casson, Alternatives to the Multinational Enterprise, Macmillan, London, 1979.

54. A series of articles written by J. H. Dunning have been published in book form, International Production and the Multinational Enterprise, Allen & Unwin, London, 1981.

55. Buckley and Casson, op.cit., p.33.

56. Ibid, pp.34-35.

57. Ibid, p.69.

58.   John H. Dunning, "Explaining Changing Patterns of International Produc-
       tion: In Defence of the Eclectic Theory", Oxford Bulletin of Economics
       and Statistics, Vol. 41, No.4, November 1979, p.275.

59.   Ibid, p.275.

60.   G. B. Richardson, "The Organisation of Industry", Economic Journal,
       Vol.82, No.327, September 1972, pp.883-884.

61.   Ibid, pp.880-890.

62.   These two forms of integration are distinguished in Kiyoshi Kojima,
       Direct Foreign Investment, op.cit., Chapter 11.

63.   John H. Dunning, "Trade, Location of Economic Activity and the MNE: A
       Search for an Eclectic Approach", in Bertil Ohlin, Per-Ore Hesselborn,
       and Per Magnus Wijkman, eds., The International Allocation of Economic
       Activity, Holmes & Meier, New York, 1977, p.401.

64.   John H. Dunning, "Explaining Changing Patterns...," op.cit, p.276.

65.   This characterisation of the trading company was made by Kiyoshi Kojima,
       Direct Foreign Investment, op.cit, Chapter 11, p.233, and "Taikaihatsu-
       tojokoku toshi no Shin Keitai" ("New Forms of Foreign Investment in
       Developing Countries"), in Yugin Kaigai Toshi Kenkyushoho (a journal
       published by the Research Center on Overseas Investment, EX-IM Bank of
       Japan, October 1981 (in Japanese).

66.   This idea is discussed in Ozawa, Multinationalism, op.cit., pp.186-188.

67.   Kojima, Direct Foreign Investment, op.cit., pp.225-227.

68.   Oliver E. Williamson, Markets and Hierarchies: Analysis and Antitrust
       Implications, Free Press, New York, 1975.

69.   Ibid., p.31.

70.   Ibid., p.26

71.   Ibid., p.37.

72.   Ibid., p.87.

73.   Ibid., p.26

74.   Alan Rugman, for example, recently declared: "The process of inter-
       nalisation explains most (and probably all) of the reasons for FDI
       (foreign direct investment). Previous writers in the literature on the
       motives for FDI have tended to identify one or more of the imperfec-
       tions in factor or product markets, or have noticed a response by the
       MNE to government induced market imperfections such as tariffs, taxes,
       and capital controls. All of these types of market imperfections serve
       to stimulate one sort of MNE or another. The MNE is in the business of
       internalising externalities. It is now time to recognise that inter-
       nalisation is a general theory of FDI and a unifying paradigm for the

theory of the MNE." "Internalisation as a General Theory of Foreign
Direct Investment: A Re-Appraisal of the Literature", <u>Weltwirtschaft-</u>
<u>liches Archiv</u>, Band 116, Heft 2, 1980, p.376.

75.   Charles Oman, <u>op. cit</u>.

OECD SALES AGENTS
DÉPOSITAIRES DES PUBLICATIONS DE L'OCDE

ARGENTINA – ARGENTINE
Carlos Hirsch S.R.L., Florida 165, 4° Piso (Galería Guemes)
1333 BUENOS AIRES, Tel. 33.1787.2391 y 30.7122

AUSTRALIA – AUSTRALIE
Australia and New Zealand Book Company Pty, Ltd.,
10 Aquatic Drive, Frenchs Forest, N.S.W. 2086
P.O. Box 459, BROOKVALE, N.S.W. 2100. Tel. (02) 452.44.11

AUSTRIA – AUTRICHE
OECD Publications and Information Center
4 Simrockstrasse 5300 Bonn (Germany). Tel. (0228) 21.60.45
Local Agent/Agent local :
Gerold and Co., Graben 31, WIEN 1. Tel. 52.22.35

BELGIUM – BELGIQUE
Jean De Lannoy, Service Publications OCDE
avenue du Roi 202, B-1060 BRUXELLES. Tel. 02/538.51.69

BRAZIL – BRÉSIL
Mestre Jou S.A., Rua Guaipa 518,
Caixa Postal 24090, 05089 SAO PAULO 10. Tel. 261.1920
Rua Senador Dantas 19 s/205-6, RIO DE JANEIRO GB.
Tel. 232.07.32

CANADA
Renouf Publishing Company Limited,
Central Distribution Centre,
61 Sparks Street (Mall),
P.O.B. 1008 - Station B,
OTTAWA, Ont. KIP 5R1.
Tel. (613)238.8985-6
Toll Free: 1-800.267.4164
Librairie Renouf Limitée
980 rue Notre-Dame,
Lachine, P.Q. H8S 2B9,
Tel. (514) 634-7088.

DENMARK – DANEMARK
Munksgaard Export and Subscription Service
35, Nørre Søgade
DK 1370 KØBENHAVN K. Tel. +45.1.12.85.70

FINLAND – FINLANDE
Akateeminen Kirjakauppa
Keskuskatu 1, 00100 HELSINKI 10. Tel. 65.11.22

FRANCE
Bureau des Publications de l'OCDE,
2 rue André-Pascal, 75775 PARIS CEDEX 16. Tel. (1) 524.81.67
Principal correspondant :
13602 AIX-EN-PROVENCE : Librairie de l'Université.
Tel. 26.18.08

GERMANY – ALLEMAGNE
OECD Publications and Information Center
4 Simrockstrasse 5300 BONN Tel. (0228) 21.60.45

GREECE – GRÈCE
Librairie Kauffmann, 28 rue du Stade,
ATHÈNES 132. Tel. 322.21.60

HONG-KONG
Government Information Services,
Publications/Sales Section, Baskerville House,
2nd Floor, 22 Ice House Street

ICELAND – ISLANDE
Snaebjörn Jónsson and Co., h.f.,
Hafnarstraeti 4 and 9, P.O.B. 1131, REYKJAVIK.
Tel. 13133/14281/11936

INDIA – INDE
Oxford Book and Stationery Co. :
NEW DELHI-1, Scindia House. Tel. 45896
CALCUTTA 700016, 17 Park Street. Tel. 240832

INDONESIA – INDONÉSIE
PDIN-LIPI, P.O. Box 3065/JKT., JAKARTA, Tel. 583467

IRELAND – IRLANDE
TDC Publishers – Library Suppliers
12 North Frederick Street, DUBLIN 1 Tel. 744835-749677

ITALY – ITALIE
Libreria Commissionaria Sansoni :
Via Lamarmora 45, 50121 FIRENZE. Tel. 579751/584468
Via Bartolini 29, 20155 MILANO. Tel. 365083
Sub-depositari :
Ugo Tassi
Via A. Farnese 28, 00192 ROMA. Tel. 310590
Editrice e Libreria Herder,
Piazza Montecitorio 120, 00186 ROMA. Tel. 6794628
Costantino Ercolano, Via Generale Orsini 46, 80132 NAPOLI. Tel. 405210
Libreria Hoepli, Via Hoepli 5, 20121 MILANO. Tel. 865446
Libreria Scientifica, Dott. Lucio de Biasio "Aeiou"
Via Meravigli 16, 20123 MILANO Tel. 807679
Libreria Zanichelli
Piazza Galvani 1/A, 40124 Bologna Tel. 237389
Libreria Lattes, Via Garibaldi 3, 10122 TORINO. Tel. 519274
La diffusione delle edizioni OCSE è inoltre assicurata dalle migliori librerie nelle
città più importanti.

JAPAN – JAPON
OECD Publications and Information Center,
Landic Akasaka Bldg., 2-3-4 Akasaka,
Minato-ku, TOKYO 107 Tel. 586.2016

KOREA – CORÉE
Pan Korea Book Corporation,
P.O. Box n° 101 Kwangwhamun, SÉOUL. Tel. 72.7369

LEBANON – LIBAN
Documenta Scientifica/Redico,
Edison Building, Bliss Street, P.O. Box 5641, BEIRUT.
Tel. 354429 – 344425

MALAYSIA – MALAISIE
University of Malaya Co-operative Bookshop Ltd.
P.O. Box 1127, Jalan Pantai Baru
KUALA LUMPUR. Tel. 51425, 54058, 54361

THE NETHERLANDS – PAYS-BAS
Staatsuitgeverij, Verzendboekhandel,
Chr. Plantijnstraat 1 Postbus 20014
2500 EA S-GRAVENHAGE. Tel. nr. 070.789911
Voor bestellingen: Tel. 070.789208

NEW ZEALAND – NOUVELLE-ZÉLANDE
Publications Section,
Government Printing Office Bookshops:
AUCKLAND: Retail Bookshop: 25 Rutland Street,
Mail Orders: 85 Beach Road, Private Bag C.P.O.
HAMILTON: Retail: Ward Street,
Mail Orders, P.O. Box 857
WELLINGTON: Retail: Mulgrave Street (Head Office),
Cubacade World Trade Centre
Mail Orders: Private Bag
CHRISTCHURCH: Retail: 159 Hereford Street,
Mail Orders: Private Bag
DUNEDIN: Retail: Princes Street
Mail Order: P.O. Box 1104

NORWAY – NORVÈGE
J.G. TANUM A/S
P.O. Box 1177 Sentrum OSLO 1. Tel. (02) 80.12.60

PAKISTAN
Mirza Book Agency, 65 Shahrah Quaid-E-Azam, LAHORE 3.
Tel. 66839

PORTUGAL
Livraria Portugal, Rua do Carmo 70-74,
1117 LISBOA CODEX. Tel. 360582/3

SINGAPORE – SINGAPOUR
Information Publications Pte Ltd,
Pei-Fu Industrial Building,
24 New Industrial Road N° 02-06
SINGAPORE 1953, Tel. 2831786, 2831798

SPAIN – ESPAGNE
Mundi-Prensa Libros, S.A.
Castelló 37, Apartado 1223, MADRID-1. Tel. 275.46.55
Libreria Bosch, Ronda Universidad 11, BARCELONA 7.
Tel. 317.53.08, 317.53.58

SWEDEN – SUÈDE
AB CE Fritzes Kungl Hovbokhandel,
Box 16 356, S 103 27 STH, Regeringsgatan 12,
DS STOCKHOLM. Tel. 08/23.89.00
Subscription Agency/Abonnements:
Wennergren-Williams AB,
Box 13004, S104 25 STOCKHOLM.
Tel. 08/54.12.00

SWITZERLAND – SUISSE
OECD Publications and Information Center
4 Simrockstrasse 5300 BONN (Germany). Tel. (0228) 21.60.45
Local Agents/Agents locaux
Librairie Payot, 6 rue Grenus, 1211 GENÈVE 11. Tel. 022.31.89.50

TAIWAN – FORMOSE
Good Faith Worldwide Int'l Co., Ltd.
9th floor, No. 118, Sec. 2,
Chung Hsiao E. Road
TAIPEI. Tel. 391.7396/391.7397

THAILAND – THAILANDE
Suksit Siam Co., Ltd., 1715 Rama IV Rd,
Samyan, BANGKOK 5. Tel. 2511630

TURKEY – TURQUIE
Kültur Yayinlari Is-Türk Ltd. Sti.
Atatürk Bulvari No : 191/Kat. 21
Kavaklidere/ANKARA. Tel. 17 02 66
Dolmabahce Cad. No : 29
BESIKTAS/ISTANBUL. Tel. 60 71 88

UNITED KINGDOM – ROYAUME-UNI
H.M. Stationery Office,
P.O.B. 276, LONDON SW8 5DT.
(postal orders only)
Telephone orders: (01) 622.3316, or
49 High Holborn, LONDON WCIV 6 HB (personal callers)
Branches at: EDINBURGH, BIRMINGHAM, BRISTOL,
MANCHESTER, BELFAST.

UNITED STATES OF AMERICA – ÉTATS-UNIS
OECD Publications and Information Center, Suite 1207,
1750 Pennsylvania Ave., N.W. WASHINGTON, D.C.20006 – 4582
Tel. (202) 724.1857

VENEZUELA
Libreria del Este, Avda. F. Miranda 52, Edificio Galipan,
CARACAS 106. Tel. 32.23.01/33.26.04/31.58.38

YUGOSLAVIA – YOUGOSLAVIE
Jugoslovenska Knjiga, Knez Mihajlova 2, P.O.B. 36, BEOGRAD.
Tel. 621.992

Les commandes provenant de pays où l'OCDE n'a pas encore désigné de dépositaire peuvent être adressées à :
OCDE, Bureau des Publications, 2, rue André-Pascal, 75775 PARIS CEDEX 16.

Orders and inquiries from countries where sales agents have not yet been appointed may be sent to:
OECD, Publications Office, 2, rue André-Pascal, 75775 PARIS CEDEX 16.

68073-10-1984

OECD PUBLICATIONS, 2, rue André-Pascal, 75775 PARIS CEDEX 16 - No. 42911 1984
PRINTED IN FRANCE
(41 84 07 1) ISBN 92-64-12644-9